From Dublin (

The Memoirs of /

1913–1925

IRISH NARRATIVES

IRISH NARRATIVES
Series edited by David Fitzpatrick

Personal narratives of past lives are essential for understanding any field of history. They provide unrivalled insight into the day-to-day consequences of political, social, economic or cultural relationships. Memoirs, diaries and personal letters, whether by public figures or obscure witnesses of historical events, will often captivate the general reader as well as engrossing the specialist. Yet the vast majority of such narratives are preserved only among the manuscripts or rarities in libraries and archives scattered over the globe. The aim of this series of brief yet scholarly editions is to make available a wide range of narratives concerning Ireland and the Irish over the last four centuries. All documents, or sets of documents, are edited and introduced by specialist scholars, who guide the reader through the world in which the text was created. The chosen texts are faithfully transcribed, the biographical and local background explored, and the documents set in historical context. This series will prove invaluable for university and school teachers, providing superb material for essays and textual analysis in class. Above all, it offers a novel opportunity for readers interested in Irish history to discover fresh and exciting sources of personal testimony

David Fitzpatrick teaches history at Trinity College, Dublin. His books include *Politics and Irish Life, 1913–1921* (1977, reissued 1998), *Oceans of Consolation: Personal Accounts of Irish Migration to Australia* (1995) and *The Two Irelands, 1912–1939* (1998).

For a full list of titles in the *Irish Narratives* series see inside front cover.

From Dublin Castle to Stormont
The Memoirs of Andrew Philip Magill
1913–1925

Edited by
Charles W. Magill

CORK UNIVERSITY PRESS

First published in 2003 by
Cork University Press
Crawford Business Park
Crosses Green
Cork
Ireland

© Cork University Press 2003

All rights reserved. No part of this book may be reprinted or reproduced or utilised by any electronic, mechanical or other means, now known or hereafter invented, including photocopying or recording or otherwise, without either the prior written permission of the Publishers or a licence permitting restricted copying in Ireland issued by the Irish Copyright Licensing Agency Ltd, The Irish Writers' Centre, 19 Parnell Square, Dublin 1.

British Library Cataloguing in Publication Data
A CIP catalogue record for this book is available from the British Library.
ISBN 1 85918 344 1
A CIP record for this publication is available from the Library of Congress.

Typesetting by Red Barn Publishing, Skeagh, Skibbereen, Co. Cork
Printed in Ireland by ColourBooks, Baldoyle, Co. Dublin

www.corkuniversitypress.com

Contents

Acknowledgements vi

Introduction 1
Editorial Note 14

The Memoirs of Andrew Philip Magill 15

Notes to Introduction 80
Notes to Narrative 82
Bibliography 89
Index 90

Acknowledgements

The preliminary work on this manuscript was done by A. P. Magill's nephew, the late Professor C. P. Magill of the University College of Wales, Aberystwyth, and he would certainly have been pleased to see it published in this form. I would like to thank Colin Harris of the Department of Western Manuscripts, Bodleian Library, University of Oxford, for letting me review A. P. Magill's private papers and for making available a copy of the full manuscript from this memoir is extracted. I am also indebted to James McGuire of the Department of Modern Irish History, University College Dublin, and his staff at the *Dictionary of Irish Biography* for helping me identify some of the figures mentioned in the narrative, and to the late Leon Ó Broin for the insights his biography of Augustine Birrell provided into the latter's character.

Introduction

Andrew Philip Magill's thirty-eight-year civil service career spanned some crucial moments in Irish and British history — the attempts to achieve land reform in Ireland, the fight for Home Rule, the First World War, the Easter Rising of 1916, the War of Independence, the Civil War, and the establishment of Northern Ireland. And many of these momentous events he was able to observe closely from his position as a civil servant and political functionary in Dublin Castle, Westminster and Belfast.

Starting as a Boy Writer in the National Education Office, he worked his way through the Police Courts, the Dublin Metropolitan Police Office in Dublin Castle, and into the Chief Secretary's Office, serving there for four years as a clerk and nine as the private secretary to the Under-Secretary, the most senior civil servant in Ireland. In 1913 he moved to Westminster as private secretary to Augustine Birrell, the erudite but reluctant Chief Secretary for Ireland,[1] with whom he developed a close relationship and for whom he clearly felt a mixture of affection and irritation at the latter's brilliance, charm and dilettantism. When Birrell resigned in the wake of his failure to foresee or forestall the 1916 Rising, they continued a correspondence for many years.

Magill, who was caught in Dublin at the time of the Rising and witnessed some of it first-hand (as did his younger brother Walter,[2] who was secretary to the Dublin Metropolitan Police), was called back to serve subsequent Chief Secretaries until 1918, when he escaped to what he hoped would be the quiet backwater of the Petty Sessions Office in Dublin. But, as the struggle for independence intensified and grew more violent, many of his courts were destroyed or closed down. And in 1921, like other Protestants in the civil service, he moved north to help establish the new government in Northern Ireland, ending up as Assistant Secretary for Home Affairs. Here, too, he was a first-hand observer of the violence, turmoil and attempts at reform that accompanied the early days of government in the North. 'We could never forget that we were sitting on a powder magazine', he wrote, 'and that any spark may cause an explosion.'[3]

At the end of his life, though he remained pessimistic about the prospects for peace and harmony between the two Irelands in his generation, he retained a deep affection and 'a positive nostalgia' for the Dublin he had left behind, the 'pleasure-loving race' that inhabited it, its natural surroundings and, in particular, for the Phoenix Park, 'the only place in Dublin which comes before me in my dreams'.[4]

Magill's forebears were of Scottish origin and came to Ireland in the seventeenth century at the time of the plantation of Ulster, settling in County Down. His grandfather, an improvident country solicitor, seems to have run through the small amount of property the family owned, and also the dowries of his two sisters, and, as A. P. Magill writes, 'was quite content to live first on my grandmother, who took over a well-known girls' school in Liverpool, and then on my father, who had little enough himself'.[5] It was in Liverpool that his father, Charles, met his mother, Marie Spengler, who had come from her native Lausanne at the age of seventeen to serve as a French governess at the school.[6]

It seems, in fact, that the women were the dominant figures in the family, for Magill writes more vividly about his mother than his father, an easygoing man who started working life as a clerk to a Dublin wholesale merchant and ended as the manager of a tobacco factory. He made many trips back to Lausanne with his mother, both as a child and in later life, and writes graphically of 'the lake with its sapphire blue, the Savoy mountains opposite, and Chillon and the Dent du Midi in the distance. It seemed like a glimpse of paradise to me and I realised then what my mother's feelings must have been when transferred from such a spot to a grimy Liverpool street.'[7] After his father's death, Marie came to live with him or with his younger brother, Walter, and followed them north when they moved to Belfast in 1921. (His older brother Charles, who seemed to have inherited some of his father's inability to handle money, joined the Indian Army and was accidentally shot in 1914, leaving behind a widow and six daughters, whom the brothers Magill helped support on their return to Ireland.)

Andrew Philip Magill was born on 6 October 1871 in Dublin, and was given a lay baptism by a Roman Catholic friend in the house at the time who feared he might not live; he was baptised again in the Presbyterian Church, to which his parents belonged, and confirmed in the Church of Ireland, to which they later switched. Thus, he would write, 'so far as outward rites are concerned, I should be fairly safe with three denominations to my name'.[8] The family lived in Drumcondra, and he attended first Bective College and then a national school, 'which laid the foundations of whatever education I subsequently acquired'.[9]

When he was sixteen, Magill passed the civil service examination for Boy Writers and was accepted for a position in the National Education Office, by his account a strange establishment whose clerks were appointed under the old nomination system. 'I can hardly imagine', he wrote, 'that there has ever been gathered together, either before or since, such a collection of cranks and oddities. The majority were younger sons or dependants of families with some political influence and who were glad to accept an appointment as copying clerk at 10d an hour.' Paydays were riotous and drunkenness rampant. He describes one Saturday when the teachers' pay envelopes were lined up in waste-paper baskets ready for dispatch and, the senior clerk being absent, the older hands brought in a supply of whiskey:

> By three o'clock, there was scarcely a sober man in the room. One genius was standing with his back to the fireplace, giving us lifelike imitations of popular Dublin preachers. Several others were stupidly drunk, while one Kerry man, whom drink seemed to excite to madness, started to show us what he called a Kerry dance, which consisted of a series of wild leaps in the air, with an earsplitting yell at each bounce, and a kick at the waste-paper baskets, so that the floor was strewn with pay envelopes like Vallombrosa. I was in terror, as I thought everyone would be dismissed, but the envelopes were picked up, the room cleared, and the culprits turned up smiling on Monday morning as if nothing had happened.[10]

Having passed the examination for Boy Clerkships in 1888, he moved on to the quieter waters of the Fisheries Office and later the Census staff. But in 1891 he was pitched back into more iniquitous surroundings when he was transferred to the Police Courts. He spent a year and a half there, watching the parade of prostitutes, pedlars and petty criminals pass before his still comparatively innocent eyes. He writes also at this time of the liveliness of the Dublin theatre scene, of the Carl Rosa Opera Company, D'Oyly Carte, and the great stage names — Sarah Bernhardt, Henry Irving, Ellen Terry, Forbes Robertson and others — who passed through, sometimes on their way to the United States via Queenstown. And he tells of fishing trips in Connemara and on the Liffey at Ballysmuttan with his brother, and bicycle expeditions — first on a boneshaker and then on a penny-farthing which he rode, astonishingly, as far as Belfast and back without thinking much of it.

After eighteen months in the Police Courts he applied for and secured a clerkship in the office of the Dublin Metropolitan Police in Dublin Castle. He spent seven years there, 'and very quiet and uneventful years they were. It was a little backwater where nothing occurred of any note.'[11] These were the years of the Parnell split,[12] which, he notes, lessened the work of the police in combating serious crime, while giving them more in keeping the peace. 'Instead of having an united party solidly against the government, and ready to condone the lawless activities of the extremists, we had two sections far too preoccupied with fighting one another to worry about an united attack on the British government.'[13]

The feuding continued after Parnell's death in 1891. 'The remaining years of the century', writes Magill, 'were full of internecine strife between the Redmondites,[14] the Healyites[15] and the Dillonites,[16] the causes of which are unknown to this day. The abuse and invective showered by one party upon the other (in which Tim Healy was *primus inter pares*) was enough to disgust any moderate man.'[17]

The Dublin Castle where he worked was a strange collection of old Queen Anne buildings and government apartments which bore no resemblance whatever to a castle and were filled with furniture which had been there for generations. 'But to the average Irishman, there was something sinister in the name. In the eyes of the populace it connoted an anti-Irish bureaucracy both extravagant and corrupt. Well I look back on it, and I remember most of the officials were appointed by competitive examinations, and were prepared to carry out faithfully the directives of their superiors, whether the latter were Home Rulers or not; and as for their being biased against the Irish, the only foundation for the charge was that they had the usual civil servants' prejudice against those who gave them extra work and trouble.'[18]

There were, however, two scandals which, in his chief's words, gave the Castle 'a sore knock'. One, which took place before his time, was revealed by William O'Brien, who edited *United Ireland*, and involved the head of the Crime Branch Special of the Royal Irish Constabulary. O'Brien published the story and was sued for libel. 'But O'Brien proved the case so conclusively that the police were forced to take action, and bring into light a series of most unsavoury scandals. I once started to read the Crown brief, a copy of which was in the library of the Chief Secretary's office. I am not mealy-mouthed, but a few pages was as far as I got. It was pitiable to think that men of rank and position could indulge in orgies which seemed to go back to the days of Heliogabalus. The judge who tried the cases told a friend that after sitting in court all day listening to the evidence, he used to go home by all the back streets as he was ashamed to look his fellow man in the eye.'[19]

The second case, known, as the Sheridan affair, involved a sergeant of that name in the RIC who was in the habit of maliciously injuring cattle and charging some unfortunate tramp with the crime. The government made the mistake of promising immunity to the constables who accompanied Sheridan if they gave evidence against him. But the promise of immunity prevented the use of the evidence, and no case could be mounted against Sheridan, who remained on the RIC payroll until he was ostracised and resigned. As a result, 'there was a cry of "Sheridan" raised in every case of cattle maiming which occurred, and the allegation was freely made that we were afraid to take action against

Sheridan and his subordinates because there was so much that might come out. As a matter of fact, in 30 years' experience, this was the only case I ever came across.'[20]

While at the Police Office, he entered Trinity College, Dublin, as an external student, working six days a week at the Castle, studying five nights a week and, among other things, having to master Greek, a compulsory subject which he had never taken at school. Hard though the work was, his years at Trinity were happy ones, and he emerged with several gold and silver medals to his credit for oratory, composition, history and political science. One odd thing struck him about his education at Trinity — it ignored Irish history altogether: 'I took an honours degree in History and Political Science, and I do not remember ever reading a line of any book dealing with Irish history. It certainly is a controversial subject and it is difficult to find any text books which are not marred by partiality, but it is strange to find the leading university in Ireland ignoring absolutely the history of Ireland.'[21]

In 1899 he was appointed to the Chief Secretary's Office in Dublin Castle and, though still a clerk, found himself at the centre of official life. For the office was the controlling department of most of the government branches in Ireland. In addition to being responsible for law and order, the Chief Secretary was president of the Local Government Board, the Department of Agriculture and the Congested Districts Board, and answered to Parliament for the Commissioners of National Education, the Land Commission, prisons, reformatories, lunatic asylums and a host of other bodies.

Four years later he moved a step closer to the centre as private secretary to the Under-Secretary for Ireland, at that time Sir Antony MacDonnell, an ex-Governor of Bengal, at first a terrifying figure, but one whose bark, he soon learned, was worse than his bite.[22] When MacDonnell retired in 1908, Magill continued in the same post under Sir James Dougherty, a former Presbyterian minister and professor at Magee College in Derry.[23] While there he encountered such celebrities as James Larkin, the firebrand labour leader with whom he crossed swords during a tramway strike;[24] Hugh Lane, whose bequest of valuable paintings forms the nucleus of Dublin's Hugh Lane Gallery to this day;[25] and W. B. Yeats and Lady Gregory, who for a time came to the Castle almost daily to protest against the Lord Lieutenant's censorship of contemporary plays[26] — 'Lady Gregory excited and voluble, Yeats looking like a Cataline conspirator and saying little'.[27] As a theatregoer himself, he watched the emergence of the Abbey Theatre and saw the controversial first productions of Synge's *The Playboy of the Western World* and Shaw's *John Bull's Other Island* and *The Shewing-up of Blanco Posnet*.

In 1913, after a brief sojourn with the Irish Land Commission, and the point at which these excerpts from his memoirs begin, he was appointed private secretary to Augustine Birrell, the current Chief Secretary and the most intriguing and important figure he would work with during his career. Birrell was appointed Chief Secretary in 1907 when he was fifty-seven years old and was a man of unusual talents. Leon Ó Broin, his biographer, wrote of him that 'Margot Asquith linked him with Chesterton, Belloc, Max Beerbohm and Bernard Shaw as men whose conversations were perpetual feasts of delight . . . He had no superior as an after-dinner speaker. In parliament he was equally impressive. His manner was unaffected and he was able to make the wittiest of observations without the suspicion of a smile.'[28] He had published biographies of Charlotte Brontë, William Hazlitt and Andrew Marvell, and produced several volumes of urbane and critical essays.

Although he served as Chief Secretary for nine years and was responsible for several important pieces of legislation, including the Irish Universities Act of 1908, the Land Act of 1909 and the Home Rule Act in 1914, and although he came to love Ireland and the Irish, he was a reluctant minister and appealed unsuccessfully on several occasions to be relieved of his post. As Magill writes, when members of the cabinet handed in their resignations to Asquith (the Prime Minister)[29] during the war in order to leave him free to remake his cabinet, Birrell said: 'It is a curious thing, Magill, I believe I am the only member of Cabinet who is really anxious to clear out, and I am the only one who will not be let go.'[30]

The Easter Rising of 1916, however, proved Birrell's undoing and precipitated his departure as the war had not. Having disregarded military demands that he crack down on the insurgents on the grounds that it 'would in my opinion be a reckless and foolish act and would promote disloyalty to a prodigious extent', he was, in his own words, staggered at the news that the Rising had taken place.[31] 'The Thing that has happened swallows up the things that might have happened had I otherwise acted.'[32] He returned to Westminster and tendered his resignation to Asquith. 'Birrell', writes Ó Broin, 'was so upset that he could not remember afterwards what words were spoken; the Prime Minister, jingling some coins in his pocket, just stood at the window and wept.'[33]

After his resignation Birrell retreated for a while to his Norfolk cottage, worked on a biography of his father-in-law, Frederick Locker-Lampson,[34] and pursued his other literary interests. In 1929 the National University of Ireland conferred on him (together with G. K. Chesterton and Hilaire Belloc) the degree of Doctor of Literature, but he was unable to receive it in person because of storms in the Irish Sea and his shaky limbs.[35]

In a letter to Magill, Birrell wrote: 'I often in my dreams visit Connemara and the mountains of Kerry, but never Dublin Castle or the Lodge. I should like to see Achill Sound again, but I do not suppose I ever shall. I should feel dull without my wife and Sir Henry Robinson[36] to drive the motor. To recapture former experiences is impossible.'[37] He died in November 1933 at the age of eighty-four, without ever revisiting the country which had ended his career.

Magill himself was in Dublin at the time of the Rising, caught at home and unable to get to Dublin Castle without a permit permitting him to cross the bridges. (Ironically, his brother, who was also trapped at home, could have got them both permits if he could have reached the Castle, since he was secretary to the Dublin Metropolitan Police.) He provides a lively account of events on the ground, supplemented by some reminiscences of his wife-to-be, Edith McTier, who was caught in the middle of the fighting.[38] Eventually a permit was sent to him, and he made his way by bicycle to Kingstown and thence back to Westminster.

After Birrell's resignation Magill was asked to continue as private secretary by Herbert Samuel, the Home Secretary, who temporarily took over the Irish Office.[39] He stayed on with Samuel's successors, H. E. Duke[40] and Edward Shortt,[41] until 1918, accompanying Duke on an extended tour of Donegal in 1917 which seems oddly carefree considering the recent and subsequent events in Ireland. It included, among other things, a trip up the Shannon in a Board of Works steamer, a sojourn at Rockingham, the imposing home of the King-Harmans, and a gargantuan and liquid lunch with the Catholic Bishop of Raphoe.[42]

Then, in July 1918, he took up the position of head of the Petty Sessions Office in Dublin, a small headquarters which supervised some 700 petty sessions clerks across Ireland and which he hoped would provide an oasis of calm after the turbulent war years in London. It was not to be. Soon what he called the campaign of 'murders and outrages' began, courthouses were destroyed, his inspectors chased out of town, government officials shot down. Although he himself was not in any danger, he did fear for his brother Walter, in a more exposed position as secretary to the Dublin Metropolitan Police.

During this period he was sent over to Westminster twice to help in the preparation of the Government of Ireland Bill, and was struck by the contempt with which cabinet ministers, no longer faced with a solid body of Nationalist MPs, treated the House. On the second occasion he was to act as liaison officer between the Irish government and Walter Long,[43] who was in charge of the Government of Ireland Bill in the House of Commons. But he found that the Chief Secretary's Office, now under Sir Hamar Greenwood,[44] ignored him, and, rather than sit idle, he asked to return to Dublin. His erstwhile chief, Augustine Birrell, summed up the Greenwood administration as follows: 'The whiteheaded boy is a great favourite in London, so we laugh and groan at the same time. But history will revile us for our cowardice and crime.'[45]

In December 1920 he married Edith McTier, and they honeymooned briefly in County Wicklow while pondering their future. The matter was soon solved when Magill was asked to go north and help establish the new government in Belfast, at first on loan and then permanently as Assistant Secretary of Home Affairs, followed soon after by his brother.

But, initially at least, Belfast was to prove no more peaceful than the city he had left, for the bloodshed followed him north, until the Civil War lured the Sinn Féin gunmen south. He writes of the government's efforts to control the lawlessness by passing a Civil Authorities Act, of its (in his view, courageous) reforms of education and liquor licensing, of the formation of the Royal Ulster Constabulary and of the need to develop Borstal institutions and convict prisons, of which Northern Ireland had none. He served for four years as Assistant Secretary before resigning in 1925 over a dispute having to do with the supply of ammunition for the RUC — he does not elaborate on this episode — and was succeeded in his post by his brother.

Magill's love mixed with exasperation for the Dublin and the Ireland that he had to leave behind are evident throughout his memoir and are reflected in the many stories of Irish life which he tells with relish and for which, unfortunately, there is no space in this narrative. Two examples must suffice. One was recounted to him by Henry Burgess,[46] Irish manager for the London and North-Western Railway:

> Burgess, who was a perfect mine of information on Ireland and things Irish, told me a story of an important American visitor who accompanied him on a visit to Co. Galway during the war. It was warm and sultry and they had been driving all day, so Burgess asked the driver if there was a cottage nearby where they could get something to drink, there being no pub close. 'Begorra, sir,' said the driver, 'there's the widow Connolly near here and she usually has something put away.'
>
> They pulled up a dilapidated thatched cottage on the roadside and the driver went in first. 'Good evening, Mrs Connolly,' he said. 'I have two gentleman here with a thirst that would trip a priest,

saving your presence, and if you could do anything for them they would be very grateful, and indeed I am not much better myself.'

'Good evening, Johnny,' replied Mrs Connolly, a withered old crone who seemed to live all alone in the cottage. 'It's true it's a very tiring day, and I am sorry that all I have is a bottle of something — I don't rightly remember its name, but I bought it with a bottle of whiskey and a dozen of stout with the money my Johnny sends me every quarter from America. My neighbours have helped me to drink the whiskey and the stout, but Peter Leyden, the publican who sold me the other bottle, said all the gentry are drinking it. So I bought a bottle, though I have never seemed to fancy it and it is here still.'

She then climbed up on a chair and out of the thatch produced a magnum of Veuve Clicquot. The American's eyes widened as he saw Burgess open the magnum and pour it into four teacups he took from the dresser. When they had gratefully finished the magnum, the old lady taking her share with the rest, Burgess wanted to pay her for the champagne. 'No, your honour,' she said, 'you did me a good turn by helping my Johnny get to America. If you don't drink it, it would only be wasted on some of my neighbours who come around every quarter as soon as they hear that Johnny's money has arrived.'

When the American got outside, he could not refrain from exclaiming about the waste and extravagance of an old woman of that class buying champagne, though, he added, 'I must say it came in very luckily for us.' He went home to America firmly convinced that most of the peasants of Connemara were living on champagne and other luxuries, quite unaware that Burgess had planted the champagne on the old woman by a trustworthy agent, and that the scene between her and the driver had all been carefully prepared solely for his mystification.[47]

The second story he tells as an example of the 'unsuspected vein of poetry' that is to be found in the practical and hardheaded Irish farmer, 'though they will rarely show it to an outsider. Sometimes, of course, the veil is lifted, but not often.' The story is as follows:

My cousin had a workman who went by the name of Paddy the Liar. He was a curious case, for he would hardly open his mouth for some months and then would embark on the wildest romance. One tale of his I remember well. He started off by saying, 'When I was working for Mr M— at Mullingar, he used to send me down to the seashore to get a load of sand.' This was a good beginning and would have delighted Charles Lamb's heart, for Mullingar is fifty miles from the sea.

'Well,' he continued, 'as I and another man were making our way down to the seashore, strolling along and not thinking of anything in particular, he suddenly says to me, "Paddy, look in the field there." I looked and I saw a mare and a foal that had no right to be there. I also saw that there was something very strange about the mare, so I says to Jimmie, "Come on, and we'll see whether we can catch the mare." Over the hedge and into the field we went, but we were not quick enough. The mare had one look at us, and took off like lightning and plunged into the sea. We were able, however, to cut off the retreat of the foal, and we grabbed it and brought it home with us triumphantly. All the while, the mare kept calling to the foal from the sea, where she was swimming until we were out of sight.

'Well, our master kept the foal and eventually put it to work. All went well until one day bad luck decided him to send the foal to fetch some sand from the seashore. We had just got a glimpse of the sea when the foal seemed to go mad and tore away, spilling Jimmie and me out of the cart. It made a mad race for the sea, into which it plunged, cart and all. We rushed down to the water's edge and luckily found a boat, which we rowed out to where the foal was. And what did we see? I declare to heaven, there was the mother biting the traces off so as to let the foal go free. She had it finished before we could interfere, and never a sign of the mare or foal did we see again.'

This [concluded Magill] was not a bad effort for a totally illiterate man. He had what the present generation, which has learned to read and write, lacks and that is the vivid imagination which enabled him

> to gather all the fragments of myths and legends which he had heard into one harmonious whole, and make them real to his mental vision.[48]

By no means a pessimist, Magill noted in the introduction to his memoirs that 'it is one of the curses of the Irish that they live in the past, and are unwilling to let the dead past bury its dead,'[49] adding that 'it is hopeless in our generation' to expect the Protestant of the North to unite with the Roman Catholic of the South and 'the only thing to do is to allow them to remain apart, and not to try and force a union upon them which can only spoil the virtues of both'.[50] It was an accurate enough assessment for his time, though perhaps he would take a more sanguine view today.

He was made a Companion of the Order of the Bath in 1919. Although he had retired before the new government offices in Stormont were ready for occupation, he got to know them well through his brother, who succeeded him as Assistant Secretary for Home Affairs, and was duly impressed at his brother's palatial room — 'far more luxurious than anything I possessed in Dublin Castle'.

He remained active in retirement, taking a law degree and being called to the bar in 1927. In his final post-retirement years he served as a temporary Resident Magistrate and chaired a commission on fisheries administration in Northern Ireland. In the late 1930s he began writing his memoirs, completing the existing draft shortly after the outbreak of the Second World War. He died on 21 April 1941, just ten days after his wife Edith, before he had time to carry out a final revision of the script. He is buried in Dundonald Cemetery, not far from Stormont, in the same grave as his wife, his mother and younger brother, W. A. Magill, who followed so closely in his footsteps.

Editorial Note

A. P. Magill's memoir is in the form of a typescript of 376 folios. After doing some initial work on it, his nephew, the late Professor C. P. Magill of the University College of Wales, Aberystwyth, presented it, together with a collection of letters from Augustine Birrell, H. E. Duke and others, to the Bodleian Library, Oxford, where it is deposited in the Department of Western Manuscripts as MS eng. c. 2803. Leon Ó Broin, Augustine Birrell's biographer, quoted from it extensively.

The original typescript is some 120,000 words in length. It covers Magill's entire lifespan and touches on many aspects of Irish life, on his travels in Ireland and abroad, London during the First World War, land reform, literature and the theatre, the legal profession and a variety of other subjects, quoting Lawrence Sterne's dictum that 'Digressions incontestably are the sunshine, they are the life and soul of reading.' Although a large proportion of this material cannot be included here, much of it is entertaining and admirably written, and I have tried to summarise it in the introduction above.

For the purposes of this narrative, I have concentrated on the period from 1913, when Magill began serving on the Chief Secretary's staff, until his retirement in 1925. Major deletions or omissions are indicated in italic, and section headings have been inserted for clarity. The original punctuation has been generally retained, as has Magill's unaccented form of the name 'Sinn Fein'. Minor errors and inconsistencies in spelling and capitalisation have been silently corrected and regularised where necessary.

The Memoirs of Andrew Philip Magill

[Bodleian Library, Oxford, MS eng. c. 2803]

[*The first half of A. P. Magill's memoirs — some 65,000 words — covers his family origins, early childhood, education and work experience, starting at the age of sixteen as a Boy Writer in the National Education Office in Dublin, moving on through the Fisheries Office, Police Courts and eventually to the Chief Secretary's Office in Dublin Castle. He also writes extensively about the social and artistic scene in the Dublin of the day, of the policemen and prostitutes, clerks and criminals he encountered during his working hours, of the holidays with his mother in her native Lausanne, of the fishing and cycling trips he took with his brother or other family members in the Dublin area or the west of Ireland. As we pick up his narrative, he is on assignment to the Irish Land Commission (or Estates Commission).*]

With Birrell in Westminster

I was very happy in the Estates Commission, and enjoyed being in an office where, if I had plenty to do, I could always take an hour off without worrying about some important things being left undone. Once the replies to the parliamentary questions had been sent over to the Castle the remainder of my work could wait a day or two if necessary and this in itself was a great relief to me. It was not to last, however, for in 1913 I was sent for to Dublin Castle and offered the private secretaryship to Mr Birrell, my predecessor, T. P. Le Fanu, having been appointed a Commissioner of Public Works. Mr Birrell was very insistent that it would only be for a few months, as he was anxious to retire, and I was so impressed with what he said that before I would accept the post I made my line of retreat safe, and was seconded from the Estates Commission with the privilege of paying my deputy £100 a year for doing my work. The salary attached to the private secretaryship was £420 a year, £120 of which was to cover the cost of living in London during the parliamentary session, and of travelling between London and Dublin. As I had to spend practically the whole year in London, I am afraid I made very little out of my salary.

However, I accepted the post, and in the autumn of 1913 I arrived in London to take up duty at the Irish Office, which consists of two houses in Old Queen St, the back of which looked out on the Birdcage Walk. They were charming old houses but quite unsuited for official purposes. I had a very fine room on the first floor with a large bow window looking out into St James' Park, while opening off it was a small room which was occupied by the Chief Secretary. I asked Sir John Taylor,[1] who had been at the Irish Office for a long time, the reason for this arrangement, and he explained to me that Mr Wyndham,[2] when Chief Secretary, had, in addition to his private secretaries, two or three unofficial helpers who used to gather together in the small room and who got in one another's way so much that Mr Wyndham finally told them to take the large room, and he would be quite content with the small one. The precedent was too good not to be followed, and the result was that I benefited thereby.

I found out very soon after my appointment that Mr Birrell was quite serious when he spoke of his early retirement. Mrs Birrell was very ill and died about a year after I joined him from some form of tumour on the brain. I never met her, but he was very attached to her, and when she had momentary spells of consciousness, she always asked for him and he was very often at the Irish Office or at the House, and could not be got at short notice. He felt this very much and he had made up his mind to retire.

I always thought it a pity that he abandoned literature for politics, to which he never really gave his heart. If he is not, perhaps, among the greatest of our English essayists, he has a place peculiarly his own. His delicacy of touch and the humour which ripples through his treatment of the most hackneyed themes make his essays a constant source of delight. Those who have tried to plough through the platitudes of Hannah More[3] can appreciate his description of how he buried her works — 19 octavo volumes in full calf — 'in a cliff facing due north with nothing between them and the Pole but leagues upon leagues of a wind-swept sea'.

You may also remember his description of the House of Commons, and his division of members of Parliament into front bench and back bench men, the former having the privilege of speaking with a table in front of them whereby they are enabled cunningly to conceal their notes, whereas the back bencher has no place in which to hide his notes except his hat, which, as Mr Birrell remarks, is a structure ill fitted for the purpose.

Mr Birrell was an extraordinarily well-read man and his real interest in life was his library. He was not a recluse, but if left to himself he would be found buried in a book in his library at Elm Park Gardens, a curious half underground room where his electric light was required even on summer afternoons. I can still see him sitting at the fire dressed in an extraordinary yellow tweed which he had got on some of his trips to the west of Ireland, with a large black cat stretched luxuriously on his knee, and with the ashes of his cigar descending gracefully on his waistcoat, immersed in some book from which I felt ashamed to distract his attention to deal with some dull problem connected with Ireland.

If he had gone then or within the next couple of years, he would have been able to say that he had held office longer than any of his predecessors, and that he had left the country quiet in his time. It was not to be, and the Irish Nationalist Party were doubly the cause of his debacle, in the first place because they insisted on him staying at his post — they would have no one else — and secondly by urging him on every occasion to do nothing, to take no notice of the murmurs of discontent which they attributed to a small number of Adullamites. I remember well, when all the members of the Cabinet handed in their resignations to Asquith during the war so as to leave him free to reconstitute the government, Mr Birrell saying to me, 'It's a curious thing, Magill, I believe I am the only member of the Cabinet who is really anxious to clear out, and I am the only one who will not be let go.' This was perfectly true as Redmond and Dillon refused to consider anyone else.

I sometimes made a feeble remonstrance as to Mr Birrell's *vis inertiae*, but his invariable answer was 'Dillon assures me it is all right and Dillon knows the country.' Well, John Dillon was a very able and sincere man, but his belief in himself amounted to megalomania, and he was unable to recognise any good in any person who opposed him. He vanished with the rest of the Nationalist Party when the real tug of war came, and I do not think Mr Birrell could have had a more untrustworthy guide. I need not throw stones, however, as we were all wrong except Bailey,[4] who kept assuring us that things were much worse than we thought.

When I arrived in London I was piloted to the Chief Secretary's room by Mr (afterwards Sir) Francis Greer,[5] our parliamentary draftsman, who introduced me to the various police on duty in the House, and from that day until I left London almost five years afterwards I was never stopped once, or questioned by any of the police. I do not know how they could know all the members of the House, and all the army of private secretaries and officials who went to and fro, but they did know them all, and never made a mistake. My particular friend was the policeman on the door which led into the actual chamber of Commons at the back of the Speaker's chair. When I was required for an Irish debate in the House, the Chief filled up a form which I sent to the Speaker who put my name on a list at the door, and it was this constable's duty to see that no unauthorised person got into the Chamber. Many a time I have run down the stairs from the Chief's room to see whether our debate was on yet, and have been greeted by my police friend with a cheerful 'You're all right, sir. Mr —— is up and he's good for twenty minutes anyhow' and I would go back, quite satisfied, as I never knew him to make a mistake.

I often wondered how the officials of the House who had to be in constant attendance stood the dreary drip of declamation. I know that one member of the press gallery told me that five minutes after a speech was made the reporter who took it down could not have told you what it was about. They acquired the habit of taking down a speech absolutely mechanically, and both eloquence and argument were wasted on them. All they valued was a slow, clear delivery which gave them no trouble. Their beau ideal of a speaker was John Redmond, who spoke slowly and with a perfect enunciation. My friend told me at the beginning of his career he complained to the chief reporter about having to take down the speech of some interminable bore. The old chief looked at him wearily and said: 'What does it matter? If one damned fool is not talking there's bound to be another.'

As for cheers or enthusiasm or even rows, the House seemed to me after my Irish training to be deadly. I was there when the House had to be adjourned owing to some great disorder during the Home Rule controversy, and except for a monotonous chant of 'vide, vide, vide,' meant for 'divide', a prayer meeting would have been as lively.

The rules of the House were very peculiar, in fact some of them seemed to me to be made by children for children. There were various rooms where no one but a member was allowed to enter, and if the Chief was in one of those places of retreat, and he was wanted for any purpose, the only thing I could do was get his parliamentary secretary to go and hunt him out. The official gallery in which we sat during debates resembled nothing so much as a church pew. It was situated at one end of the House of Commons behind the Speaker's chair, and to enter it you had to cross the lobby and climb up three or four stairs, and you then entered the gallery through a hole in the wall.

I was in the gallery one day when I saw Mr T. W. Russell[6] going out of the House by the door behind the Speaker. I was anxious to see him about some point, so I left the gallery and went down the steps and caught him in the lobby. I was discussing the point at issue with him when one of the attendants came up to me quite politely and said that I was not allowed to stand in the lobby, but when he saw me about to go out with Mr Russell, further explained that if I stood upon any of the steps leading up to the gallery, I would be on my own territory and would be all right. I thereupon solemnly stood on the lowest step, about three inches above the floor, and finished my conversation with Mr Russell at peace with all men.

One often hears complaints about the atmosphere of the House. All I can say is that I found it absolutely soporific. It reminded me of the days when I used to grind with my old schoolmaster in a classroom of the school after school hours. The room had been filled with a crowd of schoolboys and I don't think the windows were ever opened. At all events, when I had been working there for half an hour an intolerable feeling of drowsiness would come over me and I used to suffer the tortures of the damned trying to keep awake and follow what my master was saying. The only thing that saved me then was the modest amount of whiskey that usually accompanied the lesson. In the House of Commons there was no such palliative and I used to struggle with the feeling of sleep that came over me, especially when I should be listening carefully to what some member was holding forth about. However, I never disgraced myself and that was something for which I was always thankful.

It was very strange and hard work at first, but Mr Birrell's insouciance and his genial manner made it easier for me. He had appointed his clerk, a Mr Barden, as his additional private secretary, and Barden was most anxious to help in every way he could. He did not know much about Ireland, but he took charge of a branch of the work that I detested — the work connected with Mr Birrell's constituency, and in particular the sending of subscriptions to the innumerable clubs, charities and organisations of all sorts which dunned Mr Birrell for help. Mr Birrell was not a wealthy man and looked askance at these applications, and I used to chaff Barden about his habit of keeping over a batch of appeals until he could seize a favourable moment for Mr Birrell to go into them.

I did not envy him his task, for I learnt very soon that it was hopeless to try and make Mr Birrell do any work when he was not in the mood. I would spend half an hour with him in the morning and I would then see him beginning to yawn, and after another few minutes when I had got the really important things finished, I would say that the rest of the files could wait until he had more leisure, when he would jump to his feet, grasp his hat and say to me, 'I promise you, Magill, I'll come in at 10.30 tomorrow morning and we'll finish off these files then.'

Needless to say, he did no such thing, and I could rarely catch him in the House as he had several bolt holes into which he used to disappear and where I was not allowed to follow. Sir Henry Verney,[7] his Parliamentary Secretary, used to find him for me when the matter was urgent, but he was not at all grateful when he was dragged from his obscurity. On one occasion, when Redmond and Dillon wished to see him on some pressing matter, Verney eventually tracked him down, and the only thanks he got was to be told, 'Damn the fellows, I thought I had given them the slip.'

[*Here the author expatiates for some 3,750 words on some of the delegations Birrell had to receive, his lodgings and fellow lodgers in London.*]

During this time, the Home Rule controversy was going on and the feeling was very bitter. The atmosphere of the House was, to say the least, electric. Carson[8] was the heart and soul of the opposition, and even those opposed to his attitude had to admit the sincerity and wholeheartedness of his stand in defence of the Union. He was a curious figure in the House, he never wasted time on things which were not essential, but went straight to the point at issue, and when he left it there was little for the other side to say. I can see him still, tall, dark, with the massive jaw which gave him such a saturnine expression, pointing his finger at the front bench as he drove home some argument against them. He was not nearly so stern as he looked and in some ways was almost a sentimentalist. He was approached one day by an old clergyman who had known him in his salad days, and who wanted Sir Edward to appear for him in some legal matter. Sir Edward took him to the window of his chambers and said to him, 'Look out there, and you will see the chambers of a dozen men, any one of whom will be just as good as I am at dealing with your business, and whose fee will not be a fifth of mine. And in addition they will have the time to go into your case thoroughly, whereas I am too rushed with work to do justice to your case.' It was no good, in spite of everything he could say the old clergyman would have Sir Edward, no one else would do him. Carson took the case and won it to the great joy of the clergyman and refused to take a penny of his fee.

I was in the House one day when Asquith tried an old trick of his on Carson and stopping in his speech on the Home Rule Bill turned to

Carson and suddenly said to him, 'If I offer to exclude Ulster from the Home Rule Bill, will the Right Hon. and learned member accept Home Rule for the rest of Ireland?' It was a nasty question to ask on the spur of the moment. If he said yes, there would be a shout of betrayal from the southern unionists; if he said no, it laid him open to an attack from the English Liberals for his dog in the manger attitude. But Carson didn't hesitate for one minute, he jumped to his feet and said, 'If the Right Hon. member will make me a firm offer I will make him a firm answer.' This threw back on Asquith the onus which he was hoping to place on Carson, and as he was not prepared to make a firm offer he could only proceed with his speech amidst the jeers of the unionists.

Carson was a bit of a hypochondriac, and I recall Mr Birrell saying to me after some dinner at which he had been, 'I sat beside that damned fellow Carson, and he talked of nothing the whole evening but his stomach.' But on the question of the Union he was absolutely sincere, and it is no exaggeration to say that he was prepared to sacrifice health, position, and everything which men hold dear, for Ulster.

The first thing which showed the seriousness of the situation was the successful landing of a large number of rifles and other arms at Larne, north of Belfast.[9] We know now that the rifles were of various makes and that there would have been hopeless confusion as regards the ammunition, but the whole affair was managed so well and the police were so powerless that it gave us a nasty surprise. The leaders were perfectly well known, and the only proper course for the government to have followed was to have put them on trial. The government probably would never have succeeded in getting a conviction but they could have justified themselves by saying, 'We did our best, and it is not our fault if a jury in the north of Ireland sacrifices its conscience and refuses to convict.'

Instead of taking any action, the government did nothing. The Attorney-General at the time, Serjeant Moriarty[10] — afterwards Lord Justice Moriarty — had the courage of his convictions and drew up the indictment against the leaders. But Redmond and Dillon went to Asquith and asked him not to proceed which, they said, would only make martyrs of these men, and Asquith as usual decided to do nothing.

The inevitable reprisal followed, and the Redmondite volunteers proceeded to land a small cargo of arms at Howth, about nine miles from Dublin.[11] The Assistant Commissioner of the Dublin Metropolitan Police, Mr Harrel,[12] as soon as he heard of the landing, called out the military and met the volunteers marching back from Howth. He stopped them and parleyed with them, and they melted away and nothing happened. By the way, two volunteers struck across country and came to my house in a very frightened condition and asked permission to hide the guns in some safe place in the house, but my mother who had more courage than I would have had, asked them to what volunteer group they belonged, and when they said 'Redmond's', firmly replied that she would have nothing to do with them and shut the door in their faces.

Unfortunately on their way back into town, the military were jeered at and threatened by a crowd at Bachelor's Walk, and eventually fired on the crowd and several persons were killed. There was a great outcry and a commission was appointed to enquire into the whole proceedings in connection with the landing of the arms. The late Lord Shaw of Dunfermline[13] was the chairman and how he managed it I cannot say, but he secured the assent of the other two commissioners to a report which censured Mr Harrel, who had to retire. As a matter of fact I believe Mr Harrel wanted to go and his counsel, the late Sir Denis Henry,[14] was more anxious to secure his pension than to justify his action. It was commonly stated and believed that Mr Harrel would be allowed his full pension provided his defence did not embarrass the government. I can only say that Mr Powell, afterwards Mr Justice Powell,[15] who was Mr Harrel's counsel in the first place, told me that he bitterly regretted the illness which prevented his appearing, as he said he would have fought the case very differently. I could never understand why a circular sent to every junior district inspector of constabulary throughout Ireland, instructing him in the event of anyone attempting to land arms, to do exactly as Mr Harrel did — viz., to call out the military and stop the landing by force if necessary — was not referred to in the report of the Commission, as I believe the Commissioners had a copy before them. The circular was not sent to the Dublin Police simply because a landing of arms in the metropolitan district, or near it, was not considered probable.

In my opinion the dismissal of Mr Harrel was a crucial factor in disheartening the police throughout the whole of Ireland. They saw that if they did their duty they would not be supported and being human beings and not being angels, they took the safest course from that date, and refused to do anything without an order from their superior officers. I was in Mr Birrell's room in the House of Commons when he told me to send a wire suspending Mr Harrel, and in reply to a remonstrance on my part that it would mean the end of Mr Harrel, he said: 'It's no use, Magill, we must send it. Redmond and Dillon have been round at Downing St to see Asquith and he has agreed to suspend Harrel.'

Well, I have lived to see Redmond, Dillon and Asquith down and out, and none so poor as to do them reverence, while for Harrel it turned out to be the best thing that could have happened to him. The war broke out immediately afterwards, and he was appointed Intelligence Officer by the Admiralty who had the highest opinion of him and his work, and when the war was over he was made a director of Messrs Guinness, and became subsequently managing director, from which post he retired some years ago.

When Mr Birrell spoke to me about this affair I told him that the only thing for which I blamed Mr Harrel was that he let the military return through the city unaccompanied by any police. The military are of no use in a street row; the only thing they can do is to fire on the people, whereas the police are accustomed to handling crowds, and a few police armed with batons are usually more than a match for any average crowd. I was very sorry I said this, for Mr Birrell seized upon it as usual, and made it one of the charges against Mr Harrel that he had not sent back the police with the military.

[*Some 220 words omitted dealing with Lord Shaw's complaints about his subsistence allowance.*]

It was about this time that the so-called Curragh mutiny occurred.[16] There were strong rumours flying around that it was intended to send troops to the north to take action against the Ulster die-hards. At this moment, instructions were issued from the War Office to the General Officer Commanding in Ireland, directing him to enquire from the members of the Curragh garrison whether they would be prepared to proceed against the Northerns if required to do so, or whether they would prefer to resign their commissions. They were undoubtedly given the alternative, and my wife's cousin who was in the Connaught Rangers gave me a most graphic description of their colonel when the order was read out taking off his sword and laying it on the table, followed by all the other officers, who then stood around discussing what the next move in the game would be.

We had a private wire to Dublin and the War Office asked permission to use it. I had a Swiss uncle in London at the moment who had come over on official business and, as he had been very good to me in Lausanne, I had asked him to dine and go to a theatre the very evening that this all occurred. I took him out to dinner, but apologised for not being able to go to the theatre, as I explained that I had to return to the office, as this unexpected development had occurred. I then suggested that he should come back with me and sit for a while in the office where we could finish our conversation while I was not actually doing anything. He came with me and to my great surprise stayed with me till past midnight, when I decided it was time to call it a day and go home. He thanked me warmly for the most delightful evening I had afforded him. I believe he thought the procession of high officers and aides-decamp that he saw coming in and going out, and the general atmosphere of confusion and turmoil was staged for his benefit. At all events, it was a new experience for him and he assured me that no theatre could have amused and interested him as much. I was delighted to find that I had provided him with so much entertainment and as a matter of fact I had very little to do with the actual sending of the messages across the wire beyond arranging for their reception and delivery. It was not our business and I am afraid I took a certain satisfaction in seeing another department in hot water, especially as I thought the whole affair had been clumsily handled. To ask an Irish officer whether he would prefer to resign, or act against his own countrymen with whom he was probably in sympathy politically, was merely asking for trouble. Anyhow, Col. Seely[17] resigned over the incident and Mr Asquith took over the War Office temporarily.

It is curious to look back on the events of 1913 and 1914, the struggle over Home Rule, the excitement over the Curragh incident, and the gun runnings — and to remember how the outbreak of war made all our internal troubles seem so small. The murder of the Archduke [Franz] Ferdinand at Sarajevo seemed to us merely one of the incidents to which the Balkans were subject, but it soon became evident that Germany was seeking for a *casus belli*, and the skies became overcast. I shall never forget Mr Birrell saying to me after a cabinet meeting on, I think, the Friday before the declaration of war:

'It is still doubtful whether we shall go into the war or not. If we don't go in we shall be dragged in when it is too late, and in the meantime we shall earn the contempt, and justly so, of every nation in Europe. And if we do go in, it may mean the end of the British Empire.'

Then came the news of the crossing of the Belgian frontier, and all doubt was at an end. Instead of going into the war with a cabinet and a nation bitterly divided, and with a hostile minority, we went in with a unanimous resolve that we would endure to the end, and in spite of many trials and many anxious moments, we did endure and came out victorious. Two members of the cabinet resigned, John Burns[18] and John Morley,[19] but neither carried any members with him. The action of John Redmond in pledging the support of Ireland was, as Lord Grey[20] said, the one bright spot in the outlook, though it cost Redmond his position and reduced his party to a shadow of itself.

[*2,300 words omitted dealing with the war years in London, Zeppelin raids and the Armistice.*]

Easter 1916: Rebellion and Resignation

I had crossed over to Ireland with Mr Birrell on the Wednesday before Easter 1916, and I had spent Good Friday tramping over the mountains with my brother. We had arranged to go on a similar expedition on Easter Monday, but he came round on the Sunday and said his wife who had recently come home from a nursing home was not so well so he did not like to go away for the whole day; so I said to him to come to my house and we could spend the afternoon in the garden.

It was a very fine day, and we were idling about after lunch when to our surprise we saw our neighbours returning home. They had set out intending to spend the day at Howth near Dublin, and when we leaned over our garden wall and chaffed them on their early return, they told us that fighting had broken out in the streets and they could not get near the railway station. I saw that they were seriously upset, but I could not believe the truth until I heard the unmistakable sound of rifle firing in the distance and I began to realise that the rebellion had broken out. For just a week I was confined to the area in which I lived.

The city is surrounded by two canals, the Royal Canal and the Grand Canal, and the military held the bridges over them and would let no one through. My brother interviewed whoever was in charge at one of the bridges and was told that he could not get through without a permit, and in reply to his question was told that the permits were granted by the Chief Commissioner of Police at his office in Dublin Castle. It was an insoluble problem; to cross the bridge you must have a permit, and to get a permit you must cross the bridge to get at Dublin Castle, so my brother followed my example and remained where he was, awaiting developments. It was rather amusing as he was secretary to the Dublin Police and could have issued himself a permit if he could have got into his office for a moment. I was not at all anxious to get into the

Castle, as I was much safer where I was, so I let myself be turned back without making a protest. In fact one of my colleagues who lived nearby said to me that he had never seen anyone turned back so easily from his work as Magill. However, the weather was perfect and we walked up and down, talked to everybody whom we met and bought any provisions which were available. It was really very funny to meet some respectable old gentleman proudly carrying a large cabbage under his arm, and with a tin of sardines in his hand, though after the first two days the supply of everything fell short. But we were relatively lucky as regards food. On the Sunday my mother had said she must speak to Miss B———, our butcher, for sending us a huge joint of beef. There were only three of us, and it would mean that we would have to eat the beef cold and done up for the rest of the week. Before the end of the week we were very glad of the beef, and Miss B——— escaped without a word. We had also a ham in the house so we got off very well, but the shortage of bread was a very serious matter for the poor. The first supply of bread came from Belfast about a week afterwards, and had been baked in such a hurry that the loaves were all flattened and came out like griddle cakes, but they were most acceptable all the same.

What we found most disturbing was the impossibility of getting any reliable news to contradict the wild rumours that were flying around. There had been a great naval battle in which the British fleet had been wiped out, the Germans had broken through our lines, and, last but not least, a large body of Sinn Feiners were marching on Dublin from the north and would probably take our house en route. This made me very uneasy as I had overheard some men talking a short while before, and pointing out what an excellent post our house would make. There was clear ground all around it, and the roof had a parapet which would make it ideal for a look-out.

Our sole link with the outer world at this time was our milkman and his tales were melodramatic, to say the least. He described to us the state of Stephen's Green where the rebels had dug themselves in trenches, but he said the British troops had fired on them from the roofs of surrounding houses and had wiped out the occupants of one trench and 'you can see their legs sticking out of the trench, which was only a shallow affair, like posts of a wire fencing'. There was no trust to be put in his stories, but after a few days we heard that there was a newspaper to be seen in a small shop at Glasnevin, and we made our way there as quickly as possible, when we found a copy of the *Dundalk Democrat*, if I remember rightly, pasted up in a greengrocer's shop and we felt inclined to cheer when we found the British fleet was still intact and the British line was still unbroken. On the following Monday I saw British soldiers round our house to my great joy, and I heard the rebellion was over.

The most extraordinary thing to me was the way in which all the labourers and working men in the district welcomed the troops, and the savage way in which they denounced the rebels. The fact was that the shortage of food had become acute, and they had all been thoroughly frightened. If they had had their way, very few of the rebels would have been left alive, yet in the course of another week or two they had all swung round and were beginning to look upon the rebels as heroes. There were several causes for this. The first was what a friend stigmatised as 'Your damned English sense of fair play.' If the signatories of the proclamation issued by the rebels had been executed within the first twenty-four hours of their capture there would have been comparatively little feeling about it. But the long-drawn-out trials, and the execution of two today, and another two or three several days later, gave time for a feeling of sympathy to arise for them.

Then in the House of Commons, John Dillon made perhaps the most mischievous of the many violent speeches of his career, and made it in defiance of an arrangement reached by the leaders of the Nationalist Party. One of the Nationalist members told me afterwards that at a meeting of the party it was arranged that only the leaders should speak as they were afraid of what some hothead might say, and he told me John Dillon came down with a most carefully prepared speech that would have offended no one. He had scarcely begun, however, when he was interrupted and jeered at by some of the wilder Tories present, when he lost his temper, threw down his manuscript and embarked on a speech in which he referred to the rebels as heroes, and which did an infinity of harm in Ireland. Mr Asquith's visit, and his interview with the rebels, was another great mistake. It raised them in the general opinion and made them appear as patriots, and not as a mob of misguided youths who had inaugurated their movement by the cold-blooded butchery of a harmless policeman. The result of all this was that by the time the executions were over, the feeling in Ireland had changed in favour of the rebels, and the Sinn Fein movement was on its way to overthrow the old Nationalist Party.

The rebellion, though it took place at a time when the English were fighting for everything they held dear, and was aimed at stabbing them in the back, did not compare with the orgy of murder which broke out some years afterwards, or bring about the bitter feeling of helpless resentment which characterised the latter period. There were, however, some deeds connected with it which were very hard to forgive. Almost the first incident was the murder of John Brien [*recte* James O'Brien], a Dublin policeman who was on duty at the Upper Castle gate, a great, good-natured giant of a man who always had some children belonging to the Castle playing round him, and who used to give me a most exaggerated salute when I entered the Castle. On the day the rebellion started, a group of Sinn Feiners came to the Castle gate, and when he stepped out to stop them they shot him dead on the spot, although he was unarmed and they could easily have overpowered him. Then, having done this, they lost their heads and retreated, though the Castle was at their mercy and if they had entered it they could have captured the Under-Secretary, the Lord Chancellor and some of the other heads of department who had come in that morning. They went in to the office of the *Daily Express* on the opposite side of the street, and Harry Doig[21] told me when they rushed in he thought it was a joke until he saw the rifles shaking in their hands and realised that they were in such a state of nerves that anything might happen.

Then the ambush of the GRs,[22] the volunteer force generally known as the 'gorgeous wrecks', a body of men too old for war service who were used for miscellaneous duties and who were returning from a route march, suspecting no evil until a volley rang out and poor Frank Browning[23] was killed, was a wanton outrage. But the worst story I heard of the rebels' action was from my rector, who told me he was going to the Archbishop's palace in Stephen's Green on the Monday morning when he saw a barricade composed of carts overturned across the roadway. One of these carts was a laundry cart, and the contents had been spilt and were lying on the ground. One of the articles, a handkerchief was lying away from the cart, and it attracted the attention of a man who was walking or trying to walk ahead of the rector. He was hopelessly drunk even at that hour of the day, and with the persistence peculiar to a drunken man, he staggered into the street determined to pick up the handkerchief. A woman dressed in green knickerbockers called out 'Halt' but the man took no notice. The rector thought he was too drunk to hear her or grasp what she was saying if he did. The next moment she gave the order to 'Fire' and the unfortunate man fell dead in front of the barricade.

This woman was the notorious Countess Markievicz,[24] of whom Mahaffy,[25] the Provost of Trinity College, was reported to have said when he heard that she had been shown over Trinity by one of the officials of the convention which was held there in 1917, that 'if that obscene murderous whore were allowed into Trinity again he would throw the whole convention out'. I think, however, the most charitable view is that her mind was affected, and she was not entirely responsible for her actions at the end of her life. I remember an old friend in Trinity College saying to me shortly before this time, 'I tell you there is real trouble ahead of us all. The women have gone into the Sinn Fein movement *con amore*, and any movement which is largely run or influenced by women is of a far more dangerous character than where only men are concerned. Women are born rebels, and they have no sense of mercy or justice where their opinions are concerned.'

My wife (we were not married then) was part owner of a block of flats in Wilton Place and saw far more of the actual fighting than I did, for a great deal of sniping and firing went on all round her house, and the military eventually located a sniper on her roof, and after some intensive firing an officer, together with a sergeant and some men, came to her house and insisted on searching it and especially the roof. My wife brought him to the top landing from which a skylight opened on to the roof, a ladder was procured and the sergeant ordered to ascend. The officer stood beside my wife with a loaded revolver pointed at her head and refused to allow her to retreat. As she often told me, she had a vision of Percy, the name which they had given to the sniper, getting the sergeant as soon as he put his head out of the skylight, of his falling back on the officer, whose revolver would inevitably go off and kill her on the spot. However, Percy had disappeared long before the soldiers got on the roof, and all ended peaceably. Her partner in the flats, Charlie Owen, a well-known Dublin architect, had been out with the 'gorgeous wrecks' when they were ambushed, but had managed to get into a clergyman's house nearby, where he was, I will not say fitted, but clothed in some garments of his host, and he made his way to Malahide where his wife and children were staying, and where they were in great alarm, not knowing whether he was dead or alive.

My wife was told an excellent story about a lady in Gardiner Street who invited a tommy to come in, and told him there was a sniper on the roof. The tommy came in and went upstairs and looking through the skylight perceived the sniper and, taking a steady aim, shot him. The lady called up, 'Did you get him?' 'Yes,' replied the tommy. 'I got him and he has rolled down behind the parapet, but I won't go for him for fear of the military shooting me from below.' She replied, 'That is all right, then, come on down to have tea,' and she gave him an excellent tea, to which he did full credit. When he had finished, the following dialogue took place.

'How did you know the sniper was there?'

'Oh, I've known for some time.'

'Did you know who he was?'

'Yes, I know him well.'

'And who was he?'

'Just my husband.'

My wife went on the Saturday to a hastily arranged review in the College Park of the GRs and the OTC. Asquith who had come over was present at it, and there was considerable curiosity to see whether he would be booed or not. He came with the Vice-Regal party, the ladies of which were all ghastly but smiling bravely. Sir John Maxwell[26] took the salute and Asquith made no speech, so all passed off quietly, though Edith met a member of the OTC afterwards who said: 'Weren't we good? We never hissed Asquith. We wanted to, but our officers absolutely forbade it.'

The rebellion had its lighter side and I often wonder what the feelings must have been of an Englishman and his wife who took one of my wife's flats a few days before the rebellion broke out. He had explained to my wife at length that his wife's nerves had been shattered by the air raids in London, so they had determined to seek refuge in Ireland for some months where they would be free from any danger of attacks by air. It was certainly a case of out of the frying pan into the fire with a vengeance. There was also the case of an English lady, an Inspector of Factories, who was on her way to inspect a factory on Easter Monday as it would be a convenient time to look over the machinery when it was idle, and who a few minutes after leaving her hotel, saw a man fall in the street beside her hit by a stray bullet. She said to her companion who like herself was shocked at the occurrence, 'Well, I always heard the Irish were a lawless race, but I never thought they would go as far as shooting one another in a public street in this manner.'

Of course the submerged tenth of the population saw a glorious opportunity in the disturbed state of the city, and the looting that went on during the first couple of days was very bad. They showed a complete impartiality as regards the shops they broke into, and helped themselves to whatever seized their fancy, oblivious of what the politics of the owner might be. On the other hand, there were many kind and courageous acts done, which made one think more kindly of human nature than the cynics would admit. I had a friend, a son of Sir Robert Holmes,[27] who had had to give up a good career as a ladies' doctor owing to his deafness. He was fishing the Liffey about

Sallins on Easter Monday and could not get back as the trains were not running. He told me he and a number of other unfortunates were taken into houses in the village and given the best of everything. The women were given beds and the men put in front of the fire and made as comfortable as possible. The next day they walked or drove and got into Dublin somehow, when some absolute strangers whom he had met insisted on walking across town with him through some of the most dangerous districts because they said he would not hear a challenge and might be shot by mistake. I hope it will be counted to them for righteousness. It was a real danger because I had another deaf friend who had lost his hearing in South America, and who was in the Phoenix Park on the Easter Monday and was quietly strolling home, very much amazed at seeing the streets so deserted on a bank holiday, when suddenly a plate glass window of a shop front beside him went into fragments before his eyes, and he realised that something had broken out.

Another case was that of an old lady who had taken a cab on the Monday to go into town and found herself unable to return home. The cabman said there was only one thing to do and that was to come to his house which he was fortunately able to get at, and there she stayed for three or four days until it was possible to get home. They shared everything they had with her and gave up their best bed to her, and she said afterwards that none could have been kinder or more thoughtful hosts, and the old cabman refused to take anything but the cabfare, and made light of the whole business.

My wife said the thing which struck her most during the week of the rebellion was the courage and determination shown by two old ladies who shared one of the flats, and who never complained or murmured, but did everything they could to avoid giving trouble to anyone.

Our period of isolation was ended when the Chief Commissioner of Police sent an orderly out to my brother's house with a pass enabling him to get into the Castle, and he brought me out a similar pass at once. I went in to the Castle and found everything in confusion. There was waiting for me, however, a message from Mr Birrell directing me to cross to London as soon as possible, so I left Dublin Castle to look after itself, and as no other means of transport was available I cycled from my house to Kingstown, a distance of about ten miles. In the course of my journey, I must have been challenged by military patrols over a dozen times, but I reached Kingstown, left my bicycle at a friend's house and went on board the Mail boat. I sat down in the smoking room and got into conversation with a military officer who was very fierce in his denunciation of the rebels and who wound up by saying, 'The first person I would shoot is Birrell, he is responsible for the whole affair.' I did not tell him he was talking to Birrell's private secretary or he might have added me to the list.

By the way, the journey convinced me that the whole art of travelling is to do without luggage. Of course I had plenty of clothes in London, so that I did not require anything with me, but the comfort of travelling with nothing but a despatch bag, and not having to bother about getting porters or taxis made it a very pleasant journey, or it would have made it so but for the thought of what was going to happen to us all. More than ever I congratulated myself on having preserved my line of retreat as I knew that Mr Birrell's days as Chief Secretary were numbered and I felt that my days as private secretary were also probably at an end. I said to Sir Robert Chalmers,[28] who acted as Under-Secretary for a short time after Sir Matthew Nathan's[29] resignation, that when Mr Birrell resigned I must go also, but I would like to stay on for some weeks to clear up after him and sort out his personal papers. 'Ah yes,' replied Sir Robert, 'the shadow follows the substance. But take as long as you like. I know you will have plenty to do clearing up after Mr Birrell.'

I accordingly stayed on at the Irish Office for about a month reducing everything to order and collecting Mr Birrell's papers. These included the secret reports and cabinet memoranda, some of which — especially those circulated since the outbreak of war — were of vital importance. I handed them to him, and I must say that I saw them lying on the floor of his library untouched when I went to have tea with him long afterwards.

Sir Robert Chalmers (afterwards Lord Chalmers) was a big, clean-shaven, solemn-looking Englishman, but underneath his wooden exterior, he had a great sense of humour. I often met him afterwards at lunch with Sir George Stevenson,[30] the Chairman of the Board of Works, who was an old friend, and I realised not only his great ability but his rather sarcastic wit, which made his conversation distinctly entertaining. He had lost two sons in the war, which made him sympathetic with Mr Bonar Law,[31] who had suffered a similar loss, but he had a poor opinion of Lloyd George.[32] I remember during the preparations for the Irish convention I had the task of receiving the replies and forwarding them to Downing Street. Sir Robert asked me how they were coming in and had I wired the acceptances to Downing Street. I said I had sent some off and was waiting until I had a batch before sending the other replies.

'Oh no, Magill, you must not do that. If there is one thing the Goat (his name for Lloyd George) loves, it is to sit at a table and have telegrams pouring in from every side. He thinks he is doing a lot then. Put each as it comes in on the wire and do not wait until you have three or four before wiring.' Every time I went to his room after that, he used to ask me, 'Any more replies?' I would say that we had two or three, and he would say, 'Have you put them on the wire.' On my saying that I had done so, he would reply, 'That's right. Keep the wire to Downing Street red hot, and send them off the moment you get them,' and then he would chuckle to himself.

On one occasion, a chairman of a County Council called to see him on some business. On his way out, he came to my room and said in a tone of considerable exasperation: 'Mr Magill, I have been received by Mr Morley, Mr Balfour,[33] Mr Wyndham and several Under-Secretaries and they have always treated me with the utmost courtesy, but as for that b——y old Chinese mandarin that you have got in there, I don't know what to make of him.'

To anyone who knew Lord Chalmers the description was perfect. He did look like a Chinese mandarin as he sat there without any expression on his face, merely nodding at intervals to show that he was listening to what you said.

Mr Birrell gave me his photograph before he left, and I still remember the sardonic smile with which he looked at me and said, 'Shall I date it before or after the debacle, Magill?' And then he added, 'I'll put 1916 on it and that will cover both.'

I must say no one could have had a more charming chief from the personal point of view. Never out of temper, and meeting every difficulty with a jest, you could not be depressed in his company, and some periods of the war when the confidential reports from the Admiralty and the War Office which came to him as a cabinet minister were of a most pessimistic nature, were enough to depress anyone. Even on the rare occasions when he was downhearted, he could not resist a joke. One morning he said to me: 'Magill, you must get Russell to take my questions for me. There is something very wrong with me. I cannot collect my thoughts or express myself clearly and I can't face the House.'

I saw he was very much upset and said something to cheer him up. Just then Lord Wimborne[34] was shown into the room, and Mr Birrell started to tell him how ill he felt and wound up by saying: 'I am quite muddled and can't find the proper words or put an intelligible sentence together, and that damned fellow Magill says he doesn't see the least difference.' Although he was really frightened about himself, he could not resist a joke at my expense.

I must quote from his letter written to me from Biarritz after his resignation:

> I hope after returning to your old haunts at the Land Commission you have taken the advice of the Treasury official (?Sir Robert Chalmers) and gone on a few days leave during the holiday season to chew the cud of sweet and bitter remembrance, and mark the entrance of a new epoch in your own and Irish history. It has been a melancholy ending of a once cheerful song, and though personally I am out of the bog on to the dull high road, I wonder that I endured the quagmire and insincerity of the whole position. I still am sorry for my entourage, that they should have fallen with me and retired without letters after their name.

Mr Birrell, with his many good qualities, his cheerfulness and unfailing sense of humour, had some other qualities which militated against him. First of all he was lazy and he would go to more trouble avoiding any work he was called upon to do than it would have taken him to do it. As I have said elsewhere, his heart was not in his political work, and he was always anxious to get back to his library and his beloved books. I don't believe there was anyone half as anxious to retire into obscurity as he was to surrender his post as Chief Secretary.

In the second place, there was a curious vein of selfishness in his nature. His good nature did not like contemplating anything unpleasant, and he was tempted to close his eyes to anything that did not suit his views. I had an example of this when the Treasury proposed to take the rooms of our office keeper and give him an allowance for the rent of a house. This did not suit the office keeper who, beside the rooms, had free light, coal and gas. He was not as bad as another messenger who was promoted to be office keeper in a Dublin office and who was overheard by an old friend of mine recapitulating to one of his colleagues the advantages of his new position. 'You know,' he said, 'I get free coal, gas and electric light, as well as the rooms, and in addition I have control of the petty cash.' However, my office keeper asked me if I would represent to the Treasury the hardship of taking the rooms from him, and I thought it was rather hard as he had only a few years to run, and he could be left in possession for the remainder of his service. I spoke to Mr Birrell about him, and the answer I got was that I was far too sympathetic, and why should the office keeper not go?

At all events, I saw there was no use trying to get Mr Birrell to do anything and I made up my mind to let matters take their course. I was greatly surprised in a day or two when Mr Birrell came in and said to me, 'What is this nonsense about the office keeper having to give up his rooms? You must write to the Treasury and stop it, Magill.' And then he added, 'I can't have that damned woman waylaying me and weeping about their being evicted after a service of forty years.' I then saw the explanation for the mystery. The office keeper's wife had approached him and, sooner than have the task of refusing her, he had made up his mind to stop the whole thing.

Looking back on my time with Mr Birrell, while no one could ask for a more pleasant chief, I must say he took his duties very lightly. He could not be induced to make up his subject, but on the other hand he was never so good in the House as when he stood up absolutely unprepared. He would make an amusing and adroit speech, keeping the House in good humour while he skated over thin ice, and sit down without having committed himself in any way. But if we prepared a brief for him he would seldom read it, would seize on some point which we thought comparatively unimportant, and make it the mainstay of his speech, sometimes with disastrous results.

I remember well his speech on the Birrell grant in aid of the secondary teachers — the poor ushers as he always called them. I can still hear him say, 'My sympathies, Magill, are with the poor ushers,' and they certainly deserved sympathy. The lay teachers in the Roman Catholic secondary schools, which were all in the hands of religious orders, were certainly the most hardly treated, as they were only kept on until a member of the religious order could be found competent to take their place. In some of these schools, the lay teachers were dismissed after the Intermediate Examinations in June, and were taken on again in September or October, at the commencement of the new school year, so as to save paying them for three months. Mr Birrell introduced a bill making grants in aid of the salaries of secondary teachers and, as the subject was fairly complicated, Sir Francis Greer prepared a second reading speech for him which he compressed, knowing Mr Birrell's weakness, into about two foolscap pages of typewriting.

It was a masterpiece of condensation. Mr Birrell took it and I do not believe he looked at it until he was walking down to the Commons chamber. His speech was hopeless. He said everything which he ought not to have said, he got his figures all mixed up and the whole effect was deplorable. I was with him when he left the House and he said to me: 'I am afraid I made a mess of my speech,' and before I could say anything polite, he went on: 'It's all the fault of that damned Greer. How could he expect anyone to read all that stuff? If he had given me a few figures on an envelope, I would have been all right, but I could not possibly wade through the memorandum he gave me.'

I thought of poor Greer spending laborious hours with my assistance, cutting out everything which could possibly disappear, so as to get his brief down to the very bones of the subject, but I said nothing. The worst of it was that, owing to the rule that Hansard should be brought out the next day, his speech appeared in its original purity in the daily edition of Hansard. It took Greer and myself another day to amend his speech in the revised edition of Hansard, which comes out at intervals of a fortnight or so, but anyone who wishes to compare the two versions can do so, and he will perceive at once the changes that have been made. However, apparently no one took the trouble to do so, and it is ancient history now.

[*A further 660-word anecdote follows about Birrell's carelessness in the House, from which he was rescued by Sir John Taylor.*]

Staying On

Having finished with Mr Birrell, I bade all in London farewell and returned to Dublin. The next day I went into the Land Commission and reported myself for duty, when the secretary told me with a broad grin that Dublin Castle had telephoned and I was to go to the Castle as soon as I arrived. I accordingly went to the Castle where I was informed that Mr Herbert Samuel, the Home Secretary, who was to look after Ireland for the time being, had asked me to act as his private secretary for Irish affairs and handle the parliamentary questions. I agreed to act, and found myself back in the Irish Office within a few days of having left it. I was fortunate in being able to get back my old rooms, and except from the change of masters, I found little alteration in my surroundings. My new chief was, however, a great contrast to Mr Birrell. He was extraordinarily hard-working and thorough in his methods, and I soon found when I brought him a draft reply to a parliamentary question for his approval, that I must know every possible side issue that might give rise to a supplementary question. I had asked Mr Birrell once how it was that Mr Samuel, with all his great ability and industry did not carry more weight in the House, and I remember him replying, 'Oh, the infant Samuel, he is always right and the House hates a man who never makes a mistake.'

I saw the force of what Mr Birrell said now, and the reasons for Mr Samuel's omniscience. He was inclined to worry over trifles, however. There was an arrangement by which children could be transferred from one industrial school to another, and this was constantly done when the boys in a convent school got too big for the nuns in charge, and were transferred to a boys' school, usually under a religious order. The peculiarity about the system in Ireland was that the transfer orders had to be signed by the Chief Secretary. An old act of parliament mentioned the Chief Secretary and no one else, so he had to sign the orders which were purely formal as the transfers had been agreed upon by the nuns and brothers concerned. Mr Samuel, however, raised difficulties about signing these orders as he said he was not Chief Secretary. I agreed, but said there was no Chief Secretary at the moment, and in any case no question would ever be raised about the transfers. I did not tell him that when Mr Birrell was away, I used to sign his name myself.

Mr Samuel eventually signed them and I thought no more about the matter. When Mr Duke was appointed Chief Secretary some months afterwards, to my surprise a letter came to him from Mr Samuel saying he had been thinking over the matter, and in his opinion the best way out of the difficulty would be to get back the orders which he (Mr Samuel) had signed, and have fresh orders made out and signed by Mr Duke. I said to Mr Duke that whatever justification there might have been for Mr Samuel to sign these orders, there was none for Mr Duke, as the transfers had been carried out before he was appointed Chief Secretary. I need hardly say that Mr Duke agreed with me, and we heard no more of these transfers, but it seemed to me literally absurd for a man in the position of Home Secretary to be worrying himself over the transfer of little boys of seven or eight years of age from a school kept by nuns to a school kept by one of the male orders.

When Mr Duke was appointed Chief Secretary towards the end of 1916, he offered me his private secretaryship, and I was attached to the Irish Office. Mr Duke was a great lawyer [*part of sentence illegible*] and had a marvellous capacity for hard work, and he could do something which I have rarely found anyone else capable of doing. He would dictate to his shorthand writer an important document, a memorandum, for example, running to three or four pages of foolscap, and would sign it when it came back to him without altering a syllable. I, on the other hand, would tell my shorthand writer to make a rough copy and then I would proceed to alter it and put it into shape, and this is true of most men. But Mr Duke seemed to have the whole subject arranged in his head before he began to dictate it, and I presume his long training at the bar had taught him to do this.

I often quote Mr Duke as an example of how easy it is for a subordinate to spoil his chief. The first Sunday after his appointment, he came into the office on his way home from church, and opened his eyes wide when he saw me working away. 'I never dreamt', he said, 'that any civil servant worked on a Sunday.' I replied that I had come in to open any telegrams and the mailbag from Dublin to see whether there was anything urgent but that I always tried to get away before lunchtime. He expressed great surprise at this but the following Saturday he said, 'I'll look in after church and see if there is anything pressing,' and each succeeding weekend saw the same routine. He would have been quite upset if he had not found me there.

On one occasion it was distinctly fortunate that there was someone in the office on Sunday. I was working away quietly when my telephone rang and I found a very apologetic young officer speaking from the Horse Guards, who said he was very sorry to bother me on a Sunday but his chief had insisted he ring up the Irish Office and let us know what was happening. 'As a matter of fact,' he added, 'everything has been arranged in Dublin between the Under-Secretary and the General Officer Commanding in Ireland, and I don't see why we have to bother you at all.' I listened patiently, but at I last had to ask him what it was all about, and he then explained that a strike was threatened amongst the workmen employed at the electricity works at Belfast, and that the General Officer Commanding and the Under-Secretary had arranged to send a party of Royal Engineers to Belfast the next day to prevent the whole city being left without electric light or power.

I asked him whether the men were being sent as strikebreakers or merely to preserve the peace. He replied quite cheerfully that they were going to take the place of the men on strike. I told him I would get hold of the Chief as soon as I could, and telephone back later. I knew the Labour Party were bitterly opposed to the use of the military in strikes, and it did not require much imagination to see what a row would be raised in the House of Commons if it were reported that the Royal Engineers were acting as strikebreakers. I found Mr Duke at church as I expected, and he came over to the office and asked the General of Horse Guards who had insisted on ringing us up, to come across and talk the matter over. He did so and, after some discussion, it was decided to countermand the instructions given and keep the Engineers in Dublin until we could get some information on the whole question. When the General was going away, I said to him, 'It was a very fortunate thing for us, General, that you decided to phone and let us know what was proposed. My chief would have looked a perfect fool if he had been attacked in the House of Commons, and had to admit that he knew nothing of the proposal to send military to Belfast and had never been consulted in the matter at all.'

I remember his reply very well. 'My dear sir,' he said, 'I was in charge of the troops at Tonypandy and I swore a solemn oath, which I have always kept, that where the military were called in to aid the civil power, I would drag the civil power in after them as far as I possibly could.' Tonypandy was the scene of some celebrated riots in Wales some years before.

[*Some 2,500 words omitted dealing with Duke's extended tour by motor-car of Donegal in 1917.*]

I have often heard people sneer at the theory that the English cannot understand our people, but as I grow older I am more and more convinced that it is perfectly true that the two races are separated by an unbridgeable gulf. I have often told the following story as a typical example of this. I was rung up at the Irish Office one day by one of the members for Dublin city, who was a very good friend of mine, with an enquiry about labourers' cottages or something of the kind. I replied by using the stereotyped expression, dear to every civil servant's heart, that the matter was under consideration. To my surprise, he started abusing the Irish government, and informed me that he was sick of being told this, and that if we did not get a move on, he would get the party to raise hell in the House. I got annoyed and choked him off by putting the receiver down, but on thinking it over I came to the conclusion that he was playing some sort of game. I chanced to meet him in the lobby of the House that afternoon, and went up to him and said:

'Who was with you when you talked to me so peremptorily this morning?'

'Oh,' he said, 'I knew you would understand. I had so and so (mentioning the name of one of his principal supporters) beside me, and sure he thought I was talking to the Chief Secretary, and I was just letting him see how I could lay down the law to your Chief.'

I thought this a capital joke, and I could imagine the worthy supporter listening to the fearless way in which his member spoke to the Chief Secretary, little thinking that it was only a poor devil of a clerk at the other end. I went on up to Mr Duke's room, and told him about it as a good story, when to my astonishment he pulled a long face and said: 'I think it a disgraceful thing, Mr Magill, for a man in the public position of a member of parliament to be play-acting in that manner.'

I said nothing, but it gave me a shock to find how little a man who had been dealing with Irish affairs for over a year understood the Irish, or realised that we are a nation of play-actors in reality. Mr Birrell was wiser when he wrote to me (in 1933): 'We English will never understand the Irish RC race, and the sooner we part company the better. It is a thousand pities that the two islands are so near one another. I like them both.'

One of the men with whom I was brought in close contact during this period was Aubrey Herbert,[35] a younger brother of the Earl of Carnarvon and one of the most fascinating men I ever met. He was the parliamentary secretary to Mr Duke, so naturally we were in constant touch with one another. He was a wealthy man, the son of a belted earl, had been at Eton and Oxford, and yet was absolutely unspoilt. I don't know how he got out to the front, as he was so shortsighted as to be quite unfit for military service, but he was with the Irish Guards and was taken prisoner in the first days of the war. His book, *Mons, Anzac and Kut*, gives a very realistic account of his adventures.

I remember his telling me how he and two noble lords were taken prisoner in the first German rush, and how they all enlarged on their importance when cross-examined by the Germans. The French, however, were coming up and they heard the Germans deciding they would have to retreat, and debating whether they would take Herbert and the two lords with them as they seemed a prize worth holding on to. He said it was laughable how they changed their tune. He explained how he was only the younger son of a peer, and hence really a commoner; one lord said he was the younger son of a duke and the title was only a courtesy one, while the third, who was a genuine baron, could only plead that his barony was a very recent creation. However, the Germans treated them very well and left them behind to be rescued by the French.

Aubrey Herbert was the first man of his class whom I had met intimately, and he was a revelation to me. He was indifferent about money and had no idea of its real worth, and he was absolutely careless about social distinctions. He had travelled extensively in the Near East and had a wide and varied knowledge of their ways and politics, and he had a number of Balkan friends who looked to me like caricatures of the popular idea of Balkan conspirators. In spite of his harum scarum ways he had great natural ability and though he would never have made a great politician — he was too straightforward and kind-hearted — yet as an independent and trained observer who could always throw fresh light on any subject he took up he would have been extraordinarily useful, when 'came the abhorred Fury with the shears, and slit the thin spun woof of life'.

He was a peculiar colleague in many ways. If I gave him a file or a letter to read the chances were in favour of his leaving it behind somewhere, and he generally left a pair of spectacles in any place where he stayed for a few minutes, but tell him what you wanted done, and he would go off in that lighthearted way of his, and he would interview and pester everyone until he got what was required. Everyone knew him, and everyone loved him.

I was working away one day when Herbert dashed in and said excitedly, 'Have you heard the news, Magill? The Germans have landed at Dover! It's the best thing that could happen as we'll meet them on the way up and cut them to bits.' I was too astounded to say anything, but I knew he was a close friend of everyone in the cabinet and I thought he had got some exclusive information which had not reached us yet. He then asked me whether the Chief was in the office, and when I said he had not come in yet, Herbert asked me if he might use my telephone as he wanted to tell him at once. I handed him over the phone, and from the scraps of conversation I overheard, it did not sound as if things were going too well. When he put back the phone I asked him what did the Chief say. 'He asked me where did I get my information,' was the reply.

'And what did you say?' I asked, expecting the name of a cabinet minister at least.

'I said it was the butler at Lady A's where I dined last night who told me' was the paralysing reply.

'And what did the Chief say to that?' was naturally my next question.

'He said he would have me prosecuted under Dora [the Defence of the Realm Act] if I told this story to anyone else,' was Herbert's reply, and the Chief's threat seemed to afford him considerable amusement. I don't suppose there were many of Lady A's guests to whom her solemn butler would have confided his wild surmises, but it was typical of Aubrey Herbert that everyone spoke to him and told him their views and also their woes, knowing that he was one of those to whom everything that happened was full of interest. Well, he is gone, leaving a fragrant memory behind him, and we can only wonder why so full and active a life should have been cut so short, and so many others left to wither away into a useless and desolate old age.

One of the principal events of Mr Duke's comparatively short tenure of office was the setting up of the Irish convention to see whether some agreement could not be reached between the warring divisions of Irish life. It was hopeless from the start, and it was useless to expect the loyal Orangemen of the north to agree with the Sinn Feiners of the south, whom they regarded as rebels and potential assassins, and who will say now that they were wrong? It was arranged to hold the convention in the Regent House in Trinity College, Dublin. This was where we used to hold the meetings of the College Historical Society and the University Philosophical Society when I was in Trinity College. The Graduates' Memorial Building had not been erected then, and although the room was a fine one and suited for the small meetings of the societies, I had grave doubts as to whether it would do for the convention, as there was an appalling echo which would drown the voices of the speakers. However, the Board of Works took things in hand, and principally by hanging draperies from the roof, did away with the echo, and it suited the purpose admirably.

One proposal had been to hold the convention in the hall of the College of Surgeons and John Healy,[36] the editor of the *Irish Times*, came to me and said: 'You know, we are like the French, it is ridicule that kills and you can imagine what will be said about Ireland being stretched out on a dissecting table in the College of Surgeons. It will kill the convention before it starts.'

However, it was decided, as I have said, to hold it in Trinity College, and the convention was formally opened by the Chief Secretary, who wished it every good fortune and then left it to its own devices. Sir Horace Plunkett[37] was elected Chairman, principally on the advice of Sir Alexander MacDowell,[38] an Ulster solicitor and the power behind the throne of the Ulster Party. John Redmond had refused to take the chair, and there was a good deal of feeling being shown about the election, when MacDowell got up and proposed Sir Horace Plunkett as there was no strong objection to him on either side, and he thought it better to have a unanimous election than to have a bitter fight over it.

Sir Horace was an academic politician who had started life as a Unionist, but had lost the support of the true blues when he appointed T. P. Gill,[39] an ex-Nationalist Member of Parliament and a leader of the Plan of Campaign,[40] as his secretary when he was made vice-president of the department of agriculture. Sir Horace was largely responsible for the spread of cooperation amongst the Irish farmers and, although his confusing and hesitant style of speech handicapped him considerably, there is no doubt but that his views were sound, and he gave up his time and money to advocating them, receiving the usual reward in Ireland of having his house burned down during the troubles. Sir Horace was appointed Chairman and the best commentary on the situation was that of Lord MacDonnell, who said to me:

'Mr Magill, I have sat on a good many committees in my time, and of all the chairmen I have sat under, Sir Horace Plunkett was undoubtedly the worst, but he saved the situation many a time when a better man would have ruined it. When some sharp difference of opinion showed itself, and the only apparent thing to do was to take a vote which would have split the whole convention, Sir Horace would get up and say he would explain the point at issue in a few words, and at the end of half an hour, he had so befogged the situation that no one knew clearly what it was about, and we would skate over the thin ice again.'

The convention dragged along for some time before it came to an end on the question of customs and excise, but there was never really the least hope of its coming to any definite agreement. AE (George) Russell[41] resigned his seat on it some time before the final break-up, a proceeding which was commented on by Mahaffy with his usual sarcasm — 'It was very unkind of AE to desert Plunkett in this way.

Plunkett has done everything for him for the last twenty years except wash him,' a comment to which AE's untidy and hirsute appearance certainly exposed him.

With the failure of the convention ended the last hope of peace in Ireland, and from that time things went from bad to worse. It may be asked what was the cause of the anti-British spirit in Ireland. I would put first on the list the war and the terror of conscription. I remember Sir Henry Robinson saying to me during the middle of the war:

'You think you are doing a great deal by your posters about the horrors of the war at the front and the brutalities of the Germans, but I can assure you that they are having just the contrary effect to what you hope. The women are all saying they don't mind their sons and brothers being killed at home, where they can bury them and weep over them, but they won't let them go to the front where they will be blown to bits and not a scrap left to mourn over.'

The youngsters who would not enlist were determined to show that it was not fear that kept them back, and they started to drill and conspire against the English garrison.

A second cause was the discredit on which the Nationalist Party had fallen. No new blood had been introduced into it, and the role of constitutional agitation had become more and more discredited. The Catholic Church sat on the fence as usual. It was divided itself, as Maynooth, while Dr Mannix[42] was president, had turned out a number of Catholic curates who were prepared to condone all the outrages committed by the Sinn Fein Party. The late Lord Justice O'Connor[43] told me that at the first meeting of the Bishops after the murders had commenced, a pastoral condemning them in the strongest terms had been prepared, but two or three of the most extreme Bishops refused to sign it, and as always happens it was watered down until they could all sign it. He told me that Cardinal Logue[44] left the room with tears running down his cheeks at the thought of the disgrace it was for the Bishops to issue such a colourless document at such a time.

Another cause was the old theory that England's difficulty was Ireland's opportunity, and it seemed to the Sinn Fein Party that they would never again have such a chance of stabbing England in the back as at the moment when she was fighting for her life on the western front. They never took into account the fact that they are only realising now that the defeat of England would mean the end of Ireland as a nation. The old Irish hatred based on the wrongs of a century ago flared up, and they were oblivious of the consequences to themselves provided they could bring their enemy down in a common ruin.

The defeat of the rebellion drove the activities of the Sinn Feiners underground, while England was hampered at every turn by the necessity of keeping American opinion on our side. The Irish vote was a strong factor in American politics, although the American correspondent of one of our great English papers, himself an Irishman, a Roman Catholic and a nationalist, once said to me: 'What are the successes of the Irish in America? They are saloon keepers, shady lawyers and Tammany Hall politicians — while the slums of every great American city are littered with the wrecks of the Irish.' Still, their influence was a thing which had to be taken into account. England could not take real and active steps against the Sinn Feiners, and she did the worst thing she could do. She employed some time after the murder campaign started a body of ex-officers called Auxiliaries, and who were not kept under proper discipline. I know it was very hard to restrain men who were playing pitch and toss with their lives, and who sometimes saw red when they saw how their comrades were mutilated, but all the same they were allowed a licence which was inexcusable. They were a gallant crowd, however, and in spite of all the enormous difficulties in their way, they had Sinn Fein at the last gasp when Lloyd George decided to offer a peace which was all too readily accepted by the Sinn Fein Party.

One great difficulty which the Military, the Auxiliaries and the Black and Tans (who were ex-soldiers enlisted in the ordinary Royal Irish Constabulary, and were so called because when they first joined the supply of uniform trousers had run out, and they wore khaki trousers with black tunics) had to face was their want of local knowledge and their lack of confidence in the old RIC. They were Ishmaelites and they trusted no one, and this led sometimes to very awkward results. One of our Roman Catholic Resident Magistrates told me that in his district the Sinn Feiners had cut one of the main roads. The Auxiliaries turned out and commandeered all the local men to refill the trench in the road.

'I don't blame them,' he said, 'but amongst those whom they forced to work on the road in the pouring rain was the local Roman Catholic priest, a man whom I knew to have been in danger of his life for his fierce denunciation of Sinn Fein and all its works. Can you blame him if he has altered his views and is as fiercely anti-English now?'

This was a mistake which they would have avoided if they had taken an old Royal Irish Constabulary sergeant with them, but they were obsessed with the idea that every Irishman was a potential rebel and against them, and they had some justification as there were a few traitors — but only a few — at headquarters.

However, I am anticipating. Mr Duke retired to a judicial bench in March 1918 and was followed as Chief Secretary by Mr Shortt, who asked me to stay on with him. I agreed although I had been promised the appointment of Registrar of Petty Session Clerks, but the existing registrar said he would stay on as long as I wanted him to do so. Mr Shortt's first statement to me was that he had no political ambition whatsoever and that his sole desire was to follow his predecessor on to the bench as quickly as possible. He was Chief Secretary and subsequently Home Secretary, and was a decided success in both positions, but he never reached the bench, and I believe he attributed this to Lord Birkenhead,[45] who is not popular in Ireland.

I liked Mr Shortt very much. He was a man of the world, a keen fisherman, and full of life and energy. It was impossible to be dull in his company, and as regards his work, he made up his mind quickly and stuck to it. He might possibly be wrong in his views, but you knew where you were with him and need never be afraid that he would change round and let you down, which to an unfortunate private secretary is an important asset.

I stayed with him until July 1918, when I took up my post as Registrar of Petty Sessions Clerks. He wanted me to stay on and said that, if I did, he would probably get me a better post and one more worthy of me. I told him it was very kind of him to say so, but I had thought the matter out carefully. As Registrar of Petty Sessions Clerks I would be the head of a small office; I could come in when I liked and leave when I liked, within reason of course; and when I wanted a change, I could always go and inspect, at the government's expense, one of my clerks in Donegal, Connemara or Kerry, or any other beauty spot which I fancied. I said the salary would be sufficient for my modest wants, and I could see no post to which I could aspire where I would be so much my own master. Mr Shortt said it sounded like an ideal post, and he would put no difficulties in my way of accepting it.

My brother Walter was rather more brutal in his comments. His advice to me was 'Get out before you bring your chief down in the gutter, as you have done to those to whom you have hitherto been private secretary,' and there was a substratum of truth in what he said, which did not make the comment any the more appreciated.

One of the first things Mr Shortt asked me was who supplied the wine for the Chief Secretary's lodge, and when I said Jonathan Hogg he told me to ring up Mr Hogg and make an appointment to go and sample his stock. We went accordingly and I remember a lively discussion as to the hour at which the port should be decanted, one insisting that it should be decanted in the morning, the other saying that about an hour before dinner was correct. I did not join in the discussion but sipped the excellent glass of port which Jonathan Hogg gave me, and thought of my own house where the port was most probably not decanted at all, but poured straight from the bottle. I have never had any genuine taste for port which may be the real reason for my neglect of the ceremonies connected with it, and I could never see any great difference between a vintage port and the average port which one gets at a club.

Some time after my appointment as Registrar of Petty Sessions Clerks I received a letter from Mr Birrell which is so typical that I decided to include it, though it may seem rather egotistical to do so. It read as follows:

House of Commons,
November 5, 1918.

My dear Magill,

You are a pretty fellow! You have got into port (where you have assisted so many to get before you), but never a line to the storm-tossed mariner under whom you served, for whom no other port than the grave is open. I no longer peruse the Irish papers, and so until told the good news by Sir James Dougherty, I had heard nothing about it. I congratulate you heartily on being out of the Irish Office and in — anywhere else. I forget the precise nature of your duties but, whatever they may be, if you discharge them one half as well as you did those of your former office, you will be the most unpopular man in both yards.

At the moment, T.P. [O'Connor][46] is addressing an almost empty house satiated by the terms of the armistice with the dead Austro-Hungarian empire, and my successor is waiting to follow him. In a fortnight this old house will have disappeared, and with it

Your old affectionate friend and quondam chief,

Augustine Birrell

Murders and Outrages

The Petty Sessions Office of which I became the head was a curious little corner separated from the ordinary current of Irish public affairs, and was one of the few self-supporting offices in Ireland. The income derived from fines imposed at petty sessions, the fees from official documents, and from dog licences, was sufficient to pay the salaries of the petty sessions clerks and the headquarters staff, and to leave over a very fair surplus which was shared among the local authorities. With the exception of one wounded officer, who had been taken on at headquarters before I arrived, the junior of the staff was well over fifty, my predecessor was seventy-five, and my chief clerk and inspectors were close on seventy. They had all spent their lives in that small department doing the same thing day after day and I am afraid I shocked them with some of my unconventional ideas. They were, however, thoroughly loyal and when I said something to my chief clerk about feeling rather nervous about coming in as head of an office where practically every member was older than I was, and had a better claim to promotion, 'Put that idea out of your head,' was the reply. 'I never expected promotion for the Registrar has always been an outside appointment, and we are only too glad to have got you and not some old army dug out, who would have upset everything.'

[Some 1,050 words deleted dealing with the workings of the Petty Sessions Office, and some related anecdotes.]

I had told Mr Shortt before my appointment about how I was going to make a point of inspecting my clerks in all the beauty spots of Ireland, but when appointed I thought I would learn something of the work before exhibiting my ignorance. The result was that I never inspected a single clerk. Before I was at all competent to inspect any clerk, the Sinn Feiners had burnt down a number of my courthouses, and chased my inspectors out of several towns, and the whole procedure of the courts was more or less at an end. We were face to face with the worst campaign of organised murder that modern civilisation had yet witnessed, and the ordinary nature of our existence came to an end.

The murder of Alan Bell[47] was one of the deeds which brought home to us what we were up against. He was escorted to the tram, and was picked up again when he arrived in town, and escorted to Dublin Castle, but no one thought the Sinn Feiners would stop the tram, drag him out and butcher him by the roadside. This they did, and so great was the terror they inspired that two civil servants who were on the tram refused to admit that they were there or give any information to the police. I never forgot poor Mrs Alan Bell asking Sir John Taylor if Kevin Barry,[48] who was executed for taking part in another murder, was one of those who shot her husband, as she said she would die happier if she thought one of that gang had been wiped out.

This is the terrible side of all these murders and outrages, the bitter feeling they leave behind, and it is this feeling which makes rapprochement between north and south impossible so long as any of those who lived through these few years in Ireland remain. It is true that many of the leaders in what I call the murder campaign have perished, shot down in the civil war which followed the treaty, but a good many extremists are left, and some of those who used their positions under the British government to betray their comrades now hold important posts in the Free State civil service. I was not personally afraid as I held a comparatively unimportant position, but I was anxious about my brother who was secretary to the Dublin [Metropolitan] Police. However, the Dublin Police pursued a policy of masterly inactivity, and never became really obnoxious to the Sinn Feiners, although some of their more active members were murdered.

One of them was poor Hoey,[49] the detective who used to accompany the Chief Secretary when he was in Dublin. Another was Detective Sergeant John Barton,[50] an ordinary thief catcher who was involved in no political activity whatever and who was probably shot by somebody with a grudge against him. This was a feature of the Sinn Fein activities, the way in which political movements were used to cover up private animosities and hatreds.

[Here Magill digresses for about 1,700 words on contemporary accounts of the 'Troubles', which he considered less than honest, on the Irish character, and on the differences between north and south.]

After I had been some time in the Petty Sessions Office, and the Sinn Fein trouble had really begun, the British government came to the conclusion that they must do something to reduce Ireland to order, and in addition to importing the Black and Tans and the Auxiliaries, they decided to send over a number of English civil servants to show us how to run Dublin Castle. The principal of these was Sir John Anderson,[51] who was an extremely able public official and indeed so were most of the others who accompanied him, but they were quite lost in their surroundings. They lived in the Castle, ventured out very little and of course had no opportunity of getting in touch with the people, and after the peace they went back to England, unwept, unhonoured and unsung, having done little but draw large allowances for subsistence, and the risks which they were supposed to run. I am perhaps prejudiced as I came into contact with some of them over the staff of my office, and had to remind them that the Treasury had no control whatever over my office, and that the Lord Lieutenant was the head of my department to whom I threatened to appeal if any attempt was made to reduce the number or salaries of my staff.

Sir John Anderson was responsible, however, for one action which put an end to the hunger strikes. He let M[a]cSwiney,[52] the Lord Mayor of Cork who was imprisoned and went on a hunger strike, carry out the strike until he died. He survived sixty-nine days and it was commonly stated and believed that friends were allowed to bring him in provisions, as it was impossible for him to have lived for over two months without getting any sustenance. At all events he was the last hunger striker to persist in the strike. The moment that it was perceived that the government would not give way, and that the strikers would be allowed to remain without food the attempt collapsed. There was an abortive hunger strike under the Free State government but it was treated with derision by the authorities, and it collapsed almost at once.

During this time, I was sent over to London twice. On the first occasion, I went over to help Sir Francis Greer, who was overwhelmed with the work involved in the preparation of the Government of Ireland Bill, and wanted someone to relieve him on the other Irish bills which were going through the House. It was returning to my old haunts, but the first thing I felt was the change in the House of Commons. The old phalanx of Nationalist members was gone, and the result was that Ministers took no trouble at all with the preparation of their work.

I was sitting in the official gallery with Greer one day listening to the committee stage of the Government of Ireland Bill, when a clause was moved by Sir Laming Worthington-Evans,[53] who was in charge of the bill at that moment, repealing an old section of an act of George III. Sir Laming moved the clause without giving the slightest indication of what it was about, when Capt. Wedgwood Benn[54] jumped to his feet and asked what was the section enacted which it was supposed to repeal. It would have been quite sufficient for the minister to reply that it gave power to the Lord Lieutenant to suspend the Habeas Corpus act, and the House would have been quite satisfied, but it was evident that he had not the remotest idea what the clause was about, and he had not even got with him a copy of the brief which Greer had sent him the day before priming him on any debatable point. His private secretary had to get up and come round to Greer in our gallery, have a whispered consultation and then go back and explain everything to his chief. The House rose to the situation at once and cheered Wedgwood Benn when he rose again and said: 'This shows the contempt with which Ministers treat this House when they come here and ask us to pass legislation of the effect of which they have not even the foggiest idea.'

Greer turned to me and said, 'This could not have happened in the old days, when there was a real opposition. No Minister would have dared to come into the House without ever having looked at his brief, but now nobody cares.'

On another occasion, Sir Frederick Liddell,[55] the parliamentary draftsman, was in the official gallery, and I was close to him when the Minister in charge of the bill made some statements to which Sir Frederick took exception. The fact that he was not supposed to open his lips in the gallery did not make the least difference to Sir Frederick, who sat back and smiting his forehead exclaimed, 'Oh my God, he is all wrong, all wrong. Why won't Ministers read the briefs I send them? Oh, my God, he's all wrong.'

As the corner seat of the gallery which he occupied was only separated by a passage about a yard wide from the front bench, the occupants of the latter heard his remarks distinctly and all, including the Prime Minister, except the Minister whose statements were in question, gave themselves up to uncontrolled laughter.

[*There follows a 450-word anecdote about the idiosyncrasies of the House in dealing with parliamentary estimates.*]

The sense of humour of the House seemed to me a very poor thing, and they took an intense amusement out of things which left me cold, and I have often wondered whether the fault was mine or theirs. There was a parliamentary question one day about a would-be old age pensioner. The Local Government Board said that an Inspector had called on the old woman and found she had a comfortable small farm, and he went on to enumerate the livestock which she possessed — so many cows, calves, pigs, poultry etc. I struck all this out and simply said that an Inspector had called on the applicant, and found that her income was more than £31 a year (which I think was then the limit), but in going through the question with Mr Birrell he said to me: 'Oh, no, this won't do, Magill. Put all this stuff back in about the cows and calves, the pigs, cocks and hens. The House will simply love it.'

I did, of course, as he told me, and when Mr Birrell read out that the woman had three cows and two calves, the House began to laugh, when he added that she also possessed a sow and fourteen young ones, they roared with laughter, and when he came to so many cocks and hens they lay back helpless. I could not see anything very funny in the list, but it was a lesson to me that Mr Birrell's knowledge of the House and what would appeal to it was far greater than mine.

[*At this point the author discourses for some 5,000 words on other incidents which amused the House, and on the attorneys general, judges and law officers he met during his career.*]

On to Belfast

In 1920 my office in the Castle was required to house a portion of the extra police staff taken on to suppress Sinn Fein, and I was moved to Fitzwilliam St, a change which I liked as it was in quite a pleasant part of Dublin. I walked on fine days through the town and across the College Park and came home the same way. It was very pleasant to sit in the College Park on a summer afternoon, watch a cricket match and forget about the murders and mayhem that were going on outside. They were brought home to us, however, one time when a military team were playing in the Park, and some ruffian took a pot shot at one of the fielders, missed him and killed a girl who was sitting watching the match.

Another advantage of the transfer of my office was that my new address was next door to the house owned by Edith, my future wife, which she had turned into a number of flats, one of which she occupied herself. Proximity certainly hurried the course of events, and we were married in December 1920. I had only time for a short honeymoon, which we spent in Co. Wicklow, and I brought her home then to the old house in Drumcondra, which I had done up for the occasion.

After my marriage, when the state of things became steadily worse in Ireland, and when the first rumours began to spread that the English were prepared to climb down and make peace with the rebels, I discussed with my wife what our future plans would be. I determined to take my pension and leave Dublin as nothing would induce me to remain on under the men responsible for murdering so many of my colleagues. My wife said she was prepared to settle with me anywhere, but she added, 'I don't want to go to Belfast. I lived there as a child and my recollection is that I was never warm the whole time I was there. I have been back in the north many times since and I don't like the climate any better than I did as a child, and I don't care much for the people either, even though I was born and brought up in the north.'

It was tempting Providence to say this, for almost immediately I was asked if I would go north and help the new government of Northern Ireland to set up house. I accepted, and though the climate is bleak I have never regretted it. My wife had been seriously ill just after going into our house, and the Registrarship of Petty Sessions, to which I had looked forward so eagerly, had turned out anything but a haven of rest. Many of my courts were derelict, my inspectors had been chased out of the towns to which they had gone, and everything was in dire confusion. I was afraid to look at the papers in the morning lest I should see the name of a friend amongst those murdered, and I was reaching the stage of looking upon everyone with suspicion. It seemed then to get away from it all, to escape to a district where if there were murderers, there was also a powerful body able and willing to hit back, and where there were no English liberals and politicians anxious to minimise the murders and to make the most of every breach of discipline by the Black and Tans, would be only too desirable, and I accepted on the spot. To have remained in the south was impossible, and to have settled down in England was to condemn myself to being a stranger in a strange land, looked upon askance as one of the rebel Irish.

When I reached Belfast, I found that my northern ancestry, and the fact that my wife was from Co. Antrim, were a very great help to me. One agent whom my wife went to see about a suitable house was very cool in his manner, but when she mentioned that my family came from Co. Down, he became most affable, and when it turned out that his people had held some land belonging to the Magills, he wound up by saying: 'Remember, Mrs Magill, if you are in any trouble about a house, come to me and I will do anything I can to help you. It is the least I can do for a neighbour.' It is nearly one hundred years since my grandfather severed his connection with Co. Down, but the old ties still subsisted at least in the agent's mind.

[*Some 450 words omitted dealing with a civil service friend, Sam Watt, and a brief period as liaison officer in Westminster.*]

When I arrived in Belfast, I found everything in chaos. The Government had taken the Presbyterian College in College Green as a place in which to hold the meetings of Parliament, and the civil servants were packed into a few rooms in the same building. They were so congested that if anyone had to go into or out of a room everyone had to move. I can only compare it to the fifteen puzzle where you had to shift a number of pieces to get a move at all. Still we borrowed from Dublin one or two members of each department, and with their most willing help we made a start. There was some little feeling in the north about the number of Dublin civil servants who were imported, but in most cases they were from the north originally, and it was soon evident that without their help the Government could not have been carried on.

We worked early and late getting things in order and in November, 1921, orders were formally issued transferring most of the government departments to the north. I was then offered and accepted the post of Assistant Secretary to the Ministry of Home Affairs, and my wife who had remained in Dublin began to make arrangements for the move. She came to Belfast and we settled in a boarding house where she spent most of her time looking at houses and on Saturdays and Sundays we sallied forth to inspect any that she thought might prove suitable.

We had some curious experiences while house hunting. It was at the peak of the period from the owners' point of view, and in addition the Belfast landlords saw the prospect of a considerable invasion from Dublin, and determined they would not lose any of the golden harvest by asking too little. There was one house which we both fancied and although the price was high, I determined to have it. Unfortunately, or fortunately as the event proved, I mentioned to George Harris,[56] who had also come from Dublin, the fact that my wife had found the house of her dreams, and on describing to him where it was, he said: 'Oh, you mustn't take that house, Magill. I have an option on it up to the end of the present month.'

I told him I would not of course interfere, but that he had better make up his mind at once, as houses did not stay long on the market in those happy days. In a couple of days, he came to me and said that the house was withdrawn from sale as the owner had decided to stay in it. That was that, but in another month I saw the house advertised for sale again, but with £200 added to the former price. The owner had evidently come to the conclusion that, with two Dubliners after it, it was worth more than he had thought, and he had increased his price accordingly. I am glad to say we both bought other houses, and when the owner sold some years afterwards, the slump in houses had come and he dropped a large amount compared with what we would have cheerfully given him.

I had only just left Dublin when the negotiations for peace were begun which culminated in the treaty which gave the Sinn Feiners everything for which they had asked, and a great deal more than would have satisfied them. They were at the last gasp when word came that England was willing to make peace. It was the final straw, the loyalists in the south were betrayed and abandoned, and the only benefit which England obtained was temporary liberation from the eternal Irish question.

Mr Birrell gave his view of the situation in a letter he wrote to me in December 1925:

> What a medley of recollections my ten years in Ireland have provided me with. To think of all our futile wranglings over Gladstonian Home Rule, with its safeguards for the Union and the Empire, when all the time Providence had up its sleeve the repeal of the Union, to be accomplished at midnight by the leaders of the so-called Unionist party who would never hear of the least tampering with the act of Union. Well, now three-fourths of Ireland has a republic, and Craig[57] and Moore[58] govern Ulster. Let us take off our hats to the course of events which control the world.

The ink was hardly dry on the treaty before the two branches of the Sinn Fein party began fighting, and the fight is going on and will continue until the end of the British Empire. Many of the loyalists followed my example and went north, others crossed the sea and settled in England where they could bring up their children without being compelled to learn Irish, while those who could not afford to leave, stayed on and determined to support the new government as far as they could. There has been little victimisation of the Unionist minority in the south, but at first a great many appointments were given to the old adherents of Sinn Fein, many of whom were most unsuitable for their posts. I spoke some time ago to a colleague who had stayed on in the Castle and asked him how he was getting on under the Sinn Fein government.

'I can't really complain,' he said, 'but I have three men whom they appointed working in the same room with me, and their conversation is all about the raids they took part in and the police they shot during the troubles. I don't believe anything they say, they know that I served in the Great War and their idea is to irritate me so they laugh at the British soldiers and pour scorn upon the English, but it's not pleasant to have to sit there, and listen to this rot, and never say a word.'

I agreed with him that it was not pleasant and again thanked my lucky stars that I was in a land of reality and not in a land of make-believe where a mist of romance covered everything and the very vices of a bigoted and narrow-minded peasantry become the virtues of a heroic people. 'On our side is virtue and Erin, on theirs is the Saxon and the guilt.'

I never could understand the differentiation between Mr Cosgrave[59] and Mr De Valera,[60] except that Mr Cosgrave after some years of office had learnt a certain amount of sense, and had mellowed considerably, whereas Mr De Valera is a fanatic and will ever remain so. It must be remembered that the first breach in the treaty was made by Mr Cosgrave when he swept away the right of appeal to the Privy Council, and this was before the Statute of Westminster, so he could not plead that statute as an excuse. The subsequent breaches by Mr De Valera have left little standing of the original, and there is only one thing certain in the present circumstances, and that is Great Britain will not come back or have anything to do with the Irish Free State. She has got rid of it at a cost, and nothing will induce her to take up the white man's burden so far as the Free State is concerned. Why should she? She is still selling us a goodly share of her wares, she is taking from us as much as she wants, and she has no further interest in Irish affairs.

It is true that another problem has arisen. Owing to the way in which the farmers who constitute three-fourths of the Free State have been hit, a large tide of emigration to England and Scotland has flowed from the Free State, and this movement has been increased by the closing of the United States to immigrants. In many of the large English towns there is an Irish quarter and it is the same, I believe, in several

Scottish cities. There are signs of unrest in British labour circles at this problem, and if any step is taken to check this immigration, the difficulties which will arise in Ireland will be very acute. The industries which have been started are only kept alive by special tariffs, or by bounties which are paid for by the farmer, and nothing will ever make the Free State an industrial country. Agriculture is the mainstay and it must remain so. The only result of attempting to foster small industries is to make it impossible to get some things at all. A Dublin friend recently observed to me that he would not mind paying a little more to get a thing he could wear, but there were some things he could not get. He was obliged to take the home manufactured article, and it was unwearable.

What a change from the high hopes of a quarter century ago, when we were told exultantly that we would see what could be made of the Free State, liberated from dependence on England, and allowed to go her own way without hindrance. It was quite true that the Free State had a wonderful chance of becoming the most prosperous state in Europe. Freed from the burden of war debts, with a market at her door which could take all she could export, and with no necessity to keep up any military or naval expenditure, she had a happy lot indeed.

But first of all there was the civil war, which wasted millions and left an aftermath of bitterness behind it. Then places had to be found for many of those who had helped to drive out the English and a scheme of universal protection with the avowed purpose of fostering Irish industries was started, which has not paid and never will pay, and lastly the Free State fought with its only customer and lost its cattle trade during the years that the dispute about the Land Purchase annuities lasted. The net result is that the expenses and national indebtedness of the Free State have risen. By their fruits ye shall know them, and the result of twenty years' experience of the workings of the Free State does not offer any inducement to me or to anyone who is safely out of it to return.

All the same, I look back on Dublin of the pre-war days with a positive nostalgia, with something of the feeling of an old French noble to the pre-revolution days. The surroundings of Dublin on every side appealed to the wayfarer. You could wander all day long over the Dublin mountains and never tire of the views which met you at every turn of the road, or if you preferred a more limited ramble half an hour in the train landed you at Bray Head or Howth Head on opposite sides of Dublin Bay. Then within a tram ride you had what I miss most in Belfast, the Phoenix Park with its zoo and people's garden close to the entrance, its cricket and polo grounds a little further away.

I used to cycle through the Park and sit down on one of the seats high above the Liffey, 'far from the madding crowd,' and rejoice that I had so fair a scene at my disposal. It was six miles round the park and you had so much variety in those six miles that you would think the Park was of much greater extent than it really was. I have seen no public park which compares with it in its utterly unspoilt nature, and it is the only place in Dublin which comes before me in my dreams.

Then you could always find someone in Dublin to idle with you. You need never lack a companion among that pleasure-loving race for any amusement you might fancy. It may be that we were young then and that youth casts a spell over the past, but I would give a good deal to be twenty-one again and to tread the pavements of the old Dublin that I knew of yore. We were very happy then, but we did not know it. 'Those were the days', an old friend remarked to me, 'when you could go out with half-a-crown in your pocket and come home with fifteen bottles of stout under your belt.'

[*Here, for approximately 700 words, the author reminisces about life in the Dublin and Paris of his youth.*]

Northern Government, Northern 'Troubles'

In Belfast, we began to shake down after some hectic months into a more settled routine. We acquired new offices where we had more room to move, and we began to get things in order. I had said to my wife when we left Dublin: 'Well, thank Goodness, we are going to a civilised region where we won't have to jump every time a motor-car backfires.'

We arrived in Belfast and were lulled to sleep every night for the best part of a year by the sound of rifle fire and the rattle of machine guns. Fortunately the shootings were confined to well-defined areas, and our road was outside the danger zone, so we were comparatively safe. But some of the main streets, especially York Street, were very exposed to gunmen.

The streets running off York Street were Protestant and Roman Catholic quarters respectively, and snipers on both sides used to sally forth from some of these mean streets and take pot shots at their opponents on the opposite side of York Street. The result was that the ordinary law-abiding citizen whose way home lay along York Street had to take the chance of a bullet which was not meant for him at all. On a number of occasions, tram passengers had to lie down on the floor when the firing began, and got up dishevelled and dirty to curse both contending parties impartially. The police did everything in their power to stop the rioting, but it was very difficult to do so. I did not understand until I lived in Belfast the force of Sir Heffernan Considine's[61] remarks to me about the old 1888 riots, when he was the RM in charge of the Police.

'The Belfast man', he said, 'is a born street fighter, and only second in that respect to the Parisian, and then the formation of the town helps him considerably. The working men live in small streets built back to back with nothing between them but a narrow passage. You drive the crowd back into one of these streets, and they simply disappear. It is like a rabbit warren, every front and back door being left open. The crowd melts away through the houses and before you know where you are they are round at your back prepared for another attack. It is almost hopeless to keep them quiet unless you have enough men to surround the whole district.'

The same thing to some extent happened now. A man stole out of his house, took a pot shot at a man or house on the other side, and then doubled back through his own house and through his yard, and was probably in another house on a different street long before the police arrived on the scene. What made it worse was the number of gunmen from the south who descended on Belfast to carry on their old games. One of our Members of Parliament, a Mr Twaddell,[62] a most harmless individual, was shot dead in the centre of town in broad daylight, and that evening, in spite of the fact that a curfew was on, a number of men broke into a house owned by a publican and murdered the entire household. I do not know why Twaddell was murdered, and I cannot say why the publican was chosen for such a ghastly reprisal, but I know that this wave of murders sent a shiver of horror through everyone in Belfast.

I would not like to say that it put a stop to the murderous activities of the gunmen, for that would be too dreadful a thought, but it undoubtedly made them pause as they realised that they were up against a party who were just as sanguinary and evil-disposed as they were themselves. It was a different thing from shooting some unfortunate official in the south, where the general population was either in favour of the gunmen or too terrified to do anything; and the civil war breaking out at this time in the south, they decided to return to the Free State where they would have a much wider scope for their activities.

However, there was a different atmosphere then in the Free State, and I must give Cosgrave and his followers credit for tackling the situation firmly and standing no nonsense from the rebels. Rory O'Connor,[63] Erskine Childers,[64] Harry Boland,[65] Cathal Brugha,[66] and many others, where are they now? All perished and gone, and their only memorial, the ruins of Sackville St and the Four Courts have now been rebuilt, and the sole thing which recalls them is when a solicitor cannot find a deed and promptly swears an affidavit that it perished in the flames of the Four Courts.

I remember a letter in the paper suggesting that a statue should be erected in the ruins of Sackville St to Birrell and Duke with the inscription 'Arcades ambo, si monumentum requiris, circumspice.' I do not know why the writer joined Duke's name to that of Birrell — if he had put in Hamar Greenwood's name instead it would have been more appropriate. I told this story to Greer and Sir George Stevenson one day at the Irish Office, and unfortunately I gave 'circumspice' the wrong accent, whereupon my two listeners, both of whom were classical scholars, fell upon me and the humour of the story was lost in their indignation at my lapse.

Having got rid of the southern gunmen who were behind most of the outrages in the north, we settled down to comparative peace, but we could never forget that we were sitting on a powder magazine and that any spark might cause an explosion. Lord Craigavon consulted Sir Henry Wilson[67] on the general situation, and he suggested that we should employ General Solly-Flood[68] as an expert to organise the country, and act as general adviser to the Northern Government. Unfortunately, General Solly-Flood, when appointed, thought the chance too good to be lost and proceeded to get together a staff which would have done for a division at the front. He brought over a host of his own friends and put them in well-paid positions as Directors General and Assistant Directors General of various activities. Very soon we saw that if this were allowed to go on we would have an impossible bill to pay. They took an expensive house in the Malone Road for their headquarters, and of course the most lurid tales of orgies there began to circulate through Belfast, though I could never discover that there was any foundation to these stories. At all events things became impossible and finally Solly-Flood, his Directors and Assistant Directors were thanked, paid up to date and got rid of. Poor Sir Henry Wilson, of course, paid for his rashness in advising us by being murdered in London by two Irishmen, who were, however, seized by passers-by, tried and executed.

It was a great mistake on Solly-Flood's part to do as he did. If he had been content to act as adviser with one or two subordinates, he would probably be there still, drawing a handsome salary for doing nothing. Although he, personally, was quite pleasant, some of the men he brought over made themselves most objectionable, and brought his whole administration into disrepute. They did not trust the police and, of course, fell into all sorts of mistakes.

One of these was very significant. Amongst Solly-Flood's schemes was one for the defence of Northern Ireland against an attack by the Free State. When this scheme was ready, the scheme and Solly-Flood's clerk or secretary disappeared together, and there was much mutual recrimination at headquarters. It appeared that Solly-Flood had taken on this secretary, who had a good war record, without having made any enquiry about him, and the police were only too delighted to rub it in. However, he disappeared and nothing was heard of him for some years. Then the late District Inspector Lewis was on holiday in his native place in the south and called into the local police barracks to enquire about a gun which had been surrendered by his family during the troubles. He told me he was very civilly treated, and the sergeant or whoever was in charge came back after a few minutes and asked him to come in and see the Superintendent, who was anxious to see him. 'I went into the Superintendent's office, and sitting there I saw a man whose face was familiar, and who said, "Don't you remember me, Mr Lewis? I was with Solly-Flood."'

He was the missing clerk, and he told Lewis quite openly that he had copied everything that went through, but when it came to the scheme he thought it too big a thing to let slip, and he seized it and came up to Dublin with it, and he was now a superintendent of the Civic Guards. I need hardly say that this did not give us a very high impression of the secrecy of the special branch run by Solly-Flood and his henchmen, and we were glad to see them disappear.

It was a tremendous task starting a government in Northern Ireland without any chief (except the Prime Minister) who had had experience of official life. It had never occurred to me before how much the English system helped the administration of public departments. An English member enters Parliament, and after some time he gains the first step and becomes private secretary to a minister. Then, if he proves his worth, he is made parliamentary secretary to one of the departments, and after some years in harness he becomes minister of one of the lesser departments, winding up, if he is fortunate, with a seat in the Cabinet. The result is that before he attains Cabinet rank he has had a number of years in subordinate posts, learning all he can about official work, and above all learning what can be safely left to the permanent heads of the office.

Here everything was different. We had ministers and parliamentary secretaries with no experience whatever, and who wished to be consulted about everything, no matter how unimportant. Then again, a minister's friends thought they could walk in and see him at any moment, and I remember being greatly amused at the horror of one private secretary, who had gone from a big English office and was accustomed to a visitor having to get past half-a-dozen watch-dogs before he could see a minister, at the free and easy manner in which his chief's friends used to stroll into the office and go straight to his chief's room without waiting to be introduced by anyone. Belfast has all the ways of a provincial city, and I used to dread my chief's visits to his club, from which he always returned either with some absurd piece of gossip about which he wanted enquiries made at once, or with some request for a job for a hanger-on of some of his friends.

There was a tendency at first for the northerns to despise civil servants, and to imagine that anyone was competent to do their work, and they were inclined to resent the advent of trained officials from the south. That has passed away, but it did not make the beginning any easier. However, the Government, if it lacked experience, had plenty of courage; perhaps its very lack of experience increased its courage. It passed a Civil Authorities Act, much on the lines of the Defence of the Realm Act, which gave them power to deal with any disorder that might arise. The next year they tackled two of the most thorny problems they could find, passing an Education and a Licensing act.

[*The author comments here for 1,200 words on the circumstances surrounding the licensing and education reforms.*]

The Northern Government really began to function in November 1921, when the principal parts of its jurisdiction were formally transferred to it by the Imperial Government. The departments connected with law and order were handed over in deplorable condition. In most cases, the Northern Government could only get a few trained officials from each of the old departments, the Royal Irish Constabulary had been held by the Imperial Government with the threat of dismissal hanging over their heads, the Special Constabulary were only party trained and equipped, and the prisons were out of date and partly wrecked by the Sinn Fein prisoners who had been confined therein. There was neither a Borstal institution nor a convict prison in Northern Ireland.

These things were gradually remedied. A considerable number of civil servants volunteered for service in Northern Ireland, and with their help and that of ex-servicemen the nucleus of a staff for each department was formed. The Royal Ulster Constabulary was formed from old members of the force and picked members of the Special Constabulary, while the recruiting for the latter was resumed. The Government avoided the fatal mistake made by the British Government and the specials were kept under strict discipline, though it was difficult to do this with the B and C Specials, who were only an auxiliary force employed in their spare time for a nominal consideration. Still, the effort was made, the insubordinate and the unruly were weeded out and, as time went on, the Specials became more and more a force which could be relied upon to keep the peace, and to do their duty impartially.

The difficulty about convicts and Borstal inmates was got over at first by sending them to Scotland and England respectively. The Scotch prisons were quite prepared to take our prisoners at a price — and a very stiff one it was. We not only paid for the cost of maintenance of our convicts, and a proportion of the cost of the warders in Peterhead Convict Prison, but we also paid a proportion of the pensions which would ultimately be paid to these warders. However, we were very glad to get them taken over while we considered the next step.

I have spoken of the outburst of murders, and of Sinn Fein activity which occurred soon after the Northern Government was set up, and of the Act passed in response. One of the powers conferred by the act was that of interning persons who were actively opposed to the government.

A ship was purchased to be used as a place of internment — the S.S. *Argenta* — and the day after the murder of Mr Twaddell a swoop was made, and a large number of persons interned on the ship which was placed under the charge of a Mr Drysdale, who had been governor of a Scottish prison and had been recently retired on pension. He was a first-rate man for the post. He had no political leanings whatsoever, and he maintained discipline without ever having to take drastic measures. Of course, the fact that the prison was a ship moored on the lough helped, especially if the story be true that whenever the internees became unruly, he simply moved the ship out to where she met the ocean swell, and that after about an hour's rolling there was no spirit left in any of the internees.

We had some trouble with one of the internees, who was a Presbyterian and insisted that he should have a chaplain to minister to his spiritual needs. Drysdale pointed out to him that he was the only Presbyterian internee and that he could hardly expect to have a chaplain all to himself, but he added: 'I am a good Presbyterian myself, and I shall spend an hour reading the Bible to you every Sunday so that you cannot say you were neglected.' I need hardly say that the last thing which the internee wanted was an hour's tête à tête every Sunday with the governor, and we had no more complaints from him.

On another occasion, there was a hunger strike among the internees. Drysdale, passing through the dining room, saw one man who had collected three or four plates of steak in front of him, busily engaged in wolfing the steak with its accessories. Drysdale asked him what he was doing. 'I'm hunger striking, sir,' was the reply. 'I hope the strike goes on for another fortnight. I'm having the time of my life.' As a matter of fact, he overate to such an extent that the doctor had to be brought down specially to attend to him. Of course, the hunger strike petered out in a day or two. There was nothing about it in the press, and no visitors were allowed on board so that things resumed their normal course almost immediately.

A hunger strike in Belfast was defeated in a very ingenious way. A prisoner there went on hunger strike and was simply left alone, and no attempt was made to feed him forcibly. When he had been fasting for a week, the doctor — Dr O'Flaherty, who was a Roman Catholic and one of our best officials — the Governor, Major Long (author of *Tales of the RIC*), and the Chief Warder went into the cell of the prisoner, who was apparently lying unconscious. 'What do you think of him, doctor?' asked Major Long.

'I don't know,' replied the doctor. 'He is very low. He may last a day or two, but he is very likely to peg out tomorrow.'

'That will be most awkward,' said Major Long. 'Tomorrow will be Sunday, and a death in the prison on Sunday is always a nuisance. If we have to get a coffin made, that will mean more trouble as the carpenter and his assistant are off duty. What do you think, Chief?'

'If I may make a suggestion, sir,' said the Chief Warder, 'the prisoner could be measured now, and we could start the carpenter making the coffin this evening. We would then be prepared in case he does die tomorrow.'

Major Long and the doctor agreed, and the carpenter was sent for and instructed to measure the prisoner, who had lain there as if unconscious all the time. The measurements having been taken, they all left the cell, when the prisoner, who had listened with horror to these callous remarks, decided it would be wiser to resume taking his food, and the hunger strike came to a sudden end that same evening. I need hardly say the whole conversation was rehearsed beforehand by the Governor and the doctor.

[*Some sections omitted, totalling some 3,500 words, dealing with the allocation of offices, the use of informers, the sinking of the S.S.* Leinster[69] *and such family matters as travels with his mother and their household maids.*]

Shortly after I came to Belfast, my brother followed me and came to the Ministry of Home Affairs, of which I was Assistant Secretary. I cannot say what a relief it was to me to have him beside me, sharing in all the difficulties and troubles of those early years. My mother, who had stayed with us at first, went to live with him where she would have her grandson whom she adored with her, and remained with him until her death in 1924. She had had a stroke and was very feeble during the last couple of years, but her mind was not affected, and I am glad to think her last days were made as happy as possible. She was a wonderful woman, never sparing herself and careless about her personal wants, provided she could manage to give us a good start in life. But for her, my brother and I would have been nothing better than struggling clerks in a small business house.

In little more than a month after the sinking of the *Leinster,* we were rejoicing at the end of the terrible war which for four years had hung over us like a nightmare. As Mr Birrell remarked to me, 'You lie down with it at night, and in the morning when you awake, it is still with you.'

Few of us who rejoiced at the end of the Great War foresaw that before long we would be plunged into an orgy of assassination and violence which was worse in many ways than the Great War. There it was comparatively open warfare; here it was a bitter conflict in which you could not tell who was on your side or who was against you. In the end all everyone could do was to say nothing and do nothing which might attract the attention of either side. And the burnings and shooting went on until the so-called peace was made in 1921.

Even the children became demoralised. A friend heard some children playing in the street, and the game at which they were playing was the murder of Alan Bell. Her attention was directed to them by the dispute which was raging as to which of them should take the unenviable role of Alan Bell, and which should be privileged to shoot him. I thought what a pleasant way of bringing up the new generation, and what is going to become of the country. The treaty was made and the extreme republicans at once began to repudiate it until they were blown out of the Four Courts, and their leaders summarily executed. De Valera managed to keep out of the fighting, and it is curious to see how, since he has become the head of the Irish government, he has had to adopt the principles of his opponents, and has fallen out with the republicans who have not a good word to say for him.

I continued in the service of the Northern Government until 1925, when a dispute occurred as to the supply of ammunition for the Constabulary. Looking back on it, I am inclined to think that I stood too much on the letter of the law and did not make allowance for the fact that my chiefs were unaccustomed to official routine. The official who was responsible for the contract was Col. Moore, who is now Sir Thomas Moore, MP,[70] and I thought he was shabbily treated, and I determined to resign in protest. In any event, I had been overworked and harassed for a good many years, and I had reached the stage when the prospect of doing nothing except what I wished was almost irresistible. I accordingly took my pension, as I was entitled to do under the Government of Ireland Act, and settled down to a lazy life.

I soon found the monotony of an idle life after a strenuous one was too much, and I determined to get called to the Bar. I was called in 1927, and while I cannot say it was a very lucrative move, I must say I found the library and the members of the Bar made a very pleasant club, and I was still youthful enough in my outlook to appreciate the jests and good-natured chaff which the members enjoyed at one another's expense.

I may explain for the benefit of the Saxon that our system at the Bar in Ireland is different from that which obtains in England. Here all members, both silks and stuff gownsmen, work together in a common library, and the assembled barristers form a true democracy, gathering around the fire to listen to the latest story which spares no one. If we trace the origin of the various good stories which circulated through Dublin, and it is the same in Belfast, only that the humour is a little attenuated, we shall find they all came out of the Law Library. Then the Circuits were an excellent means of taking a holiday with a good crowd. Those who had no briefs, and I had only one in my various circuits, went and played golf, or fished, or amused themselves in some way, and all met for dinner in the evening which sometimes became rather festive. On one occasion during the troubles one of our barristers who had the reputation of not having gone to bed sober for forty years and who was, nevertheless, the first up in the morning, was dining with the judges who always occupy the Judges' lodgings, and who did not put up with the members of the Bar. As it was during the troubles, a military car and escort were told off to drive him and the other guests to and from the Judges' lodgings. The difficulty was that when they reached Omagh on the return journey, poor S, who had done himself extra well, was unable to tell the driver where he was staying. The other members of the Bar were ignorant of his address — he stayed with friends in Omagh — and they were at a regular impasse, when a bright idea struck one of them. Drive up to the steps of the Courthouse and put S on the steps with his back to the Courthouse, and see what happens. It worked perfectly for instinct, or whatever you may please to call it, came into play and S made for his home like a homing pigeon.

My unique case amused me. It was a writ against a sub-sheriff for the illegal seizure of a calf. A good deal turned on the identification of the calf, which had been castrated. I still remember the utter bewilderment of the witness, a stolid farmer, when the judge — Danny Wilson[71] — asked him if he had noticed any alteration in the expression of the calf after it had undergone this painful operation. The Crown Solicitor was dining with the judges that evening and he referred to this case as 'Magill's ewe lamb', when Danny interrupted him and said, 'It was not a ewe lamb, it was a bull calf.'

I got a certain amount to do helping to form an index to the statutes and aiding the Parliamentary Draftsman to draft certain bills, which kept me fairly occupied and broke the sudden change from a busy life to a life of leisure. It was a pleasant change in many ways. I could lie in my bed in the morning and come down to breakfast at ten o'clock without any sense of guilt, and on the other hand I could work as late as I liked. I was master of my own fate and that, to one who had been so many years at the beck and call of others, was a luxury in itself.

My brother had succeeded me in the office, and eventually became Secretary to the Ministry for Home Affairs. Although he was very well treated, and liked the position, he was determined to retire on pension as soon as he could, and enjoy his *dolce far niente*. He had his calendar marked and counted the days until the date of his retirement. If ever a man had greatness thrust upon him, it was my brother for, left to himself, he would have remained in a subordinate position, and would have shunned the responsibility and worry which was attached to the post of Secretary. He was, however, marked out for promotion, and accepted the post when it was offered him. He was a very conscientious and able official but, as he often said to me, 'I mean to follow you into retirement at the first possible opportunity, Phil,' and he carried out his intention for the day he turned sixty was the day of his retirement, or his release as he termed it.

It was in April, 1939, that he retired and the plans that we had made as to how we would enjoy our leisure have all gone agley, as a few months after he retired, the present war broke out, and we have not the heart to amuse ourselves while the new generation is plunged into the inferno to fight once more for the maintenance of liberty and freedom of thought in the world.

Notes to Introduction

1   Augustine Birrell (1850–1933), politician and writer; Chief Secretary for Ireland from 1907 to 1916 in the Liberal governments of Campbell-Bannerman and Asquith; essayist and biographer of note, whose name inspired the verb 'to birrell', meaning to comment on life gently and allusively.
2   Walter Alexander Magill (1879–1950). He followed his brother into the Civil Service as a Boy Clerk and joined the Dublin Metropolitan Police Office in 1898, becoming Secretary and Accountant of the Board in 1921. After the Anglo-Irish Treaty of 1921 he became Principal Clerk, Ministry of Home Affairs, in Ulster. He succeeded his brother as Assistant Secretary to the Ministry and became Permanent Secretary in 1935, retiring in 1939.
3   Magill, Memoirs, f. 343.
4   Ibid., ff. 338–9.
5   Ibid., ff. 15–16.
6   Charles Magill (1841–1909) and Marie (Spengler) Magill (1846–1924).
7   Magill, Memoirs, f. 79.
8   Ibid., f. 12.
9   Ibid., f. 23.
10 Ibid., ff. 49–51.
11 Ibid., f. 110.
12 Charles Stewart Parnell (1846–91), Home Rule politician and president of the Irish National Land League, and later of the National League; leader of the Irish Parliamentary Party until deposed under pressure from Gladstone's Liberal government in 1890.
13 Magill, Memoirs, f. 124.
14 John Edward Redmond (1856–1918), leader of the Irish Parliamentary Party, 1900–18.
15 Timothy Michael Healy (1855–1931), Nationalist and MP from 1880 to 1918; headed the revolt against Parnell in 1890–91 and became an Independent Nationalist; he served as the first Governor-General of the Irish Free State (1922–28).
16 John Dillon (1851–1927), Nationalist MP from 1880 to 1918 and supporter first of Parnell and then of Redmond; he succeeded Redmond as leader in 1918.
17 Magill, Memoirs, f. 123.
18 Ibid., f. 128.
19 Ibid., f. 130.
20 Ibid., f. 131.
21 Ibid., f. 146.
22 Sir Antony Patrick MacDonnell (1844–1925), civil servant and statesman; appointed Permanent Under-Secretary in Dublin Castle in 1902; resigned in 1908 and created Baron MacDonnell of Swinford.

Notes to Introduction

23 Rt Hon. Sir James Brown Dougherty (1844–1934), appointed Assistant Under-Secretary for Ireland in 1895 and Under-Secretary in 1908; retired in 1914 and elected unopposed as Liberal MP for Londonderry City.

24 James Larkin (1874–1947), labour leader and organiser of the Irish Transport and General Workers' Union. After the general strike of 1913 he was jailed briefly for sedition and then went to the United States to raise funds for the Irish cause.

25 Sir Hugh Percy Lane (1875–1915), Irish art collector, critic and director of the National Gallery of Ireland. He was drowned when the *Lusitania* was torpedoed in 1915.

26 W. B. Yeats (1865–1939) and Lady Gregory (Isabella Augusta Gregory (1852–1932), the Irish playwright at whose country house Yeats wrote many of his poems) were co-founders of the Irish Literary Theatre and later the Abbey Theatre.

27 Magill, Memoirs, f. 194.

28 Leon Ó Broin, *The Chief Secretary: Augustine Birrell in Ireland* (London, 1969), p. 3.

29 Herbert Henry Asquith, 1st Earl of Oxford and Asquith (1852–1928), Liberal Prime Minister, 1908–16.

30 Magill, Memoirs, ff. 222–3.

31 Leon Ó Broin, *Dublin Castle and the 1916 Rising* (Dublin, 1966), p. 66.

32 Ó Broin, *Chief Secretary*, p. 175.

33 Ibid., p. 176.

34 Frederick Locker-Lampson (1821–95), English author remembered for his light verse in *London Lyrics* and other volumes. Birrell edited his memoirs and completed a biography of him in 1920.

35 Ó Broin, *Chief Secretary*, pp. 205–13.

36 Rt Hon. Sir Henry Augustus Robinson, 1st Bart (1857–1927), Vice-President of the Local Government Board for Ireland, 1898–1922. He usually accompanied Chief Secretaries on their tours of Ireland.

37 Magill, Memoirs, f. 92.

38 Edith McTier, whom Magill married in 1920, was co-owner of a block of flats in Wilton Place which was the focus of sniping and military action for a full week. She also was owner of a small doll factory nearby which was searched by soldiers. She left a twenty-page typewritten account of the week's events.

39 Herbert Louis Samuel, 1st Viscount Samuel (1870–1963), Liberal politician, philosopher and administrator. He resigned as Home Secretary when Lloyd George supplanted Asquith in December 1916, but subsequently held office in several administrations.

40 Rt Hon. Henry Edward Duke (1855–1939), Conservative and Unionist politician; Chief Secretary for Ireland, 1916–18; created Baron Merrivale in 1925.

41 Edward Shortt (1862–1935), Liberal politician; Chief Secretary for Ireland, 1918–19; Home Secretary, 1919–22.

42 Patrick O'Donnell (1856–1927), Bishop of Raphoe, 1888–1922; Archbishop of Armagh, 1924–27; created cardinal in 1925.

43 Rt Hon. Walter Hume Long (1854–1924), Unionist politician; President of the Local Government Board for England, 1900–5 and 1915–16; Chief Secretary for Ireland, 1905; Chairman of the Irish Unionist Party, 1906–10; created Viscount Long of Wraxall in 1921.

44 Rt Hon. Sir Hamar Greenwood (1870–1948), Chief Secretary for Ireland 1920–22; a member of the British delegation which negotiated the Anglo-Irish Treaty, 1921; created Baron Greenwood in 1929 and Viscount Greenwood in 1937.

45 Magill, Memoirs, f. 334.

46 Rt Hon. Henry Givens Burgess (1859–1937), Shipping and Coal Controller (Ireland), 1917–19; Director-General of Transportation (Ireland), 1919; nominated member of Seanad Éireann, 1922–28.

47 Magill, Memoirs, ff. 192–4.

48 Ibid., ff.154–5.

49 Ibid., f. 10.

50 Ibid., f. 5.

Notes to Narrative

1 Sir John James Taylor (1859–1945). He held a variety of posts in the Irish Office from 1892 to 1920, including that of Principal Clerk in the Chief Secretary's Office, 1911–18; Assistant Under-Secretary, 1918–20.

2 Rt Hon. George Wyndham (1863–1913), Unionist politician and man of letters; Chief Secretary for Ireland, 1900–5.

3 Hannah More (1745–1833), dramatist, poet, Christian moralist, and pioneer of universal education.

4 Rt Hon. William Frederick Bailey (1857–1917), Estates Commissioner under the Irish Land Act of 1903 and one of the Irish Land Commissioners.

5 Sir Francis Nugent Greer (1869–1925), Parliamentary Draftsman, Irish Office, 1908–23; Parliamentary Counsel to the Treasury, 1923–25.

6 Thomas Wallace Russell (1841–1920), Liberal politician. He supported Home Rule after 1900 and founded the New Land Movement in Ulster, advocating compulsory purchase. Created 1st Baronet in 1917.

7 Sir Henry Calvert Williams Verney (1881–1974), Liberal politician; Parliamentary Private Secretary to Augustine Birrell, 1911–14; Parliamentary Secretary to

the Minister of Agriculture and Fisheries, 1914–15; Assistant Director of Labour with the British Expeditionary Force, 1916.

8   Sir Edward Henry Carson (1854–1935), MP for Dublin University, 1892–1918, and for Duncairn (Belfast), 1918–21; prominent barrister and leader of the Irish Unionist Party, 1910–21; created 1st Baron Carson of Duncairn in 1921.

9   On 24 April 1914, 800 Ulster Volunteers cordoned off the harbour at Larne and unloaded 25,000 rifles and 2,000,000 rounds of ammunition, which they then dispersed in the countryside.

10 Rt Hon. John Francis Moriarty (d. 1915), First Serjeant-at-Law for Ireland, 1910–13; Solicitor General for Ireland, May–June 1913; Attorney General for Ireland, 1913–14; Lord Justice of Appeal in Ireland, 1914–15.

11 On 26 July 1914 the Irish Volunteers landed 900 rifles and 26,000 rounds of ammunition at Howth.

12 William Vesey Harrel (1866–1956), District Inspector, RIC, 1886–98; Inspector of Prisons in Ireland, 1898; Assistant Commissioner, Dublin Metropolitan Police, 1902–14; Temporary Commander, Royal Navy Volunteer Reserve, 1915–19.

13 Rt Hon. Thomas Shaw (1850–1937), lawyer and politician; Solicitor General for Scotland, 1894–95; Lord Advocate, 1905–9; Lord of Appeal with life peerage, 1909–29; created Baron Craigmyle in 1929.

14 Rt Hon. Sir Denis Stanislaus Henry (1864–1925), Solicitor General for Ireland, 1918–19; Attorney General for Ireland 1919–21; Lord Chief Justice of Northern Ireland (though a Roman Catholic), 1921.

15 Rt Hon. Mr Justice John Blake Powell (d. 1923), judge of the High Court of Justice in Ireland, Chancery Division.

16 The Curragh 'mutiny' took place in March 1914 when a cabinet committee recommended moving troops from the south of Ireland and England to help protect depots in the north against the Ulster Volunteers. When threatened with dismissal should they decline to participate in these military operations in Ulster, fifty-eight cavalry officers at the Curragh military base near Kildare opted for resignation with the prospect of dismissal.

17 Maj.-Gen. Rt Hon. John Edward Bernard Seely (1868–1947), politician and soldier; Secretary of State for War, 1912–14, he resigned after the Curragh 'mutiny'; created Baron Mottistone in 1933.

18 Rt Hon. John Elliot Burns (1858–1943), labour leader and politician; President of the Board of Trade in 1914, he resigned from the cabinet in the belief that war could have been avoided.

19 Rt Hon. John Morley (1838–1923), author and Liberal politician; Chief Secretary for Ireland, 1886 and 1892–95; Secretary of State for India 1905–10; Lord President of the Council, 1910–14, he resigned when Great Britain entered the war; created Viscount Morley of Blackburn in 1908.

20 Rt Hon. Sir Edward Grey (1862–1933), Secretary of State for Foreign Affairs, 1905–16; Ambassador to Washington, 1919–20; created 1st Viscount Grey of Fallodon in 1916.

21 Henry Stuart Doig (1874–1931), barrister-at-law and editor of the *Dublin Daily Express and Evening Mail*; expelled from the office of the *Evening Mail* by the insurgents, who seized and held it for thirty hours.

22 Their official name was the Dublin Veterans' Volunteer Corps, but they were commonly known as the 'GRs' because of the words 'Georgius Rex' sewn on their armlets.

23 F. H. Browning, the commander of the GR company and former president of the Irish Rugby Football Union, was shot in the spine and subsequently died in hospital. The GRs were unable to return fire because they had no ammunition for their ancient Italian rifles.

24 Countess Constance Georgine de Markiewicz (1878–1927), nationalist activist and founder of Na Fianna Éireann, a republican youth organisation. She was condemned to death after the 1916 Rising, but her sentence was commuted to life imprisonment and she was released under the general amnesty of 1917.

25 Professor Sir John Pentland Mahaffy (1839–1919), Provost of Trinity College, Dublin, 1914–19; knighted in 1918.

26 General Rt Hon. Sir John Grenfell Maxwell (1859–1929), commander of the British forces during the 1916 Rising. He was given complete control of the country under martial law, executed fifteen rebels and detained thousands of others. His handling of the crisis was widely criticised, but was defended by Asquith.

27 Sir Robert William Arbuthnot Holmes (1843–1910), Irish barrister; Treasury Remembrancer and Deputy Paymaster for Ireland, 1882–1908.

28 Sir Robert Chalmers (1858–1938), civil servant and administrator; Governor of Ceylon, 1913–16; Joint Permanent Secretary to the Treasury, 1916–19; Under-Secretary for Ireland, 1916; Master of Peterhouse, Cambridge, 1924–31; created Baron Chalmers of Northiam in 1919.

29 Sir Matthew Nathan (1862–1939), civil servant and administrator; Governor of the Gold Coast, 1900–3; Governor of Hong Kong, 1903–7; Governor of Natal, 1907–9; Secretary to the Post Office, 1909–11; Chairman, Board of Inland Revenue, 1911–14; Under-Secretary for Ireland, 1914–16; Secretary, Ministry of Pensions, 1916–19; Governor of Queensland, 1920–25.

30 Sir George Augustus Stevenson (1856–1931), Private Secretary to W. L. Jackson, Chief Secretary for Ireland, 1891–92; Commissioner of Public Works, Ireland, 1892–1913; Chairman of the Board of Public Works, Ireland, 1913–21.

31 Andrew Bonar Law (1858–1923), leader of the Unionist Party from 1911, and a member of the War Cabinet; Prime Minister, October 1922 – May 1923.

Notes to Narrative 85

32 David Lloyd George (1863–1945), Welsh Liberal statesman; Prime Minister, 1916–22; created 1st Earl Lloyd-George of Dwyfor in 1945.

33 Arthur James Balfour (1848–1930), Chief Secretary for Ireland, 1887–91; Conservative Prime Minister, 1902–5; created 1st Earl of Balfour in 1922.

34 Ivor Churchill Guest, 2nd Baron Wimborne (1873–1939), Conservative and later Liberal MP; Lord Lieutenant of Ireland, 1915–18; created 1st Viscount Wimborne in 1918.

35 Hon. Aubrey Nigel Henry Molyneux Herbert (1880–1923), second son of the 4th Earl of Carnarvon; honorary attaché in Tokyo (1902) and Constantinople (1904); war service in France, Egypt, Gallipoli, Mesopotamia and Salonika; Parliamentary Secretary to H. E. Duke, Chief Secretary for Ireland, 1916–18.

36 John Edward Healy (1872–1934), Editor of the *Irish Times*, 1907–34; called to the Irish bar in 1906.

37 Sir Horace Curzon Plunkett (1854–1932), pioneer of agricultural co-operation; Unionist MP for South County Dublin, 1892–1900; Chairman of Irish Convention, 1917–18; founded Irish Dominion League, 1919; nominated member of Seanad Éireann, 1922–23.

38 Sir Alexander MacDowell (d. 1917), Belfast solicitor; government nominee to Irish Convention, 1917.

39 Thomas Patrick Gill (1858–1931), Nationalist politician, journalist and civil servant, who served on numerous agricultural bodies both before and after the establishment of the Irish Free State.

40 The Plan of Campaign: an organised stratagem employed by tenants against selected landowners between 1886 and 1891 in an effort to reduce rents.

41 George William Russell, better known by his pseudonym AE (1867–1935), poet, painter and editor of the *Irish Homestead*, 1906–23, and *Irish Statesman*, 1923–30.

42 Daniel Mannix (1864–1963), President of St Patrick's College, Maynooth, 1903–12; Archbishop of Melbourne, 1917–63.

43 Rt Hon. Charles Andrew O'Connor (1854–1928), Solicitor General for Ireland, 1909–11; Attorney General for Ireland, 1911–12; Master of the Rolls in Ireland, 1912–24; judge of the Supreme Court, Irish Free State, 1924–25.

44 Michael Logue (1840–1924), Bishop of Raphoe, 1879–87; Archbishop of Armagh, 1887–1924; created cardinal in 1893. A supporter of the Gaelic League, he opposed Sinn Féin but supported the Anglo-Irish Treaty of 1921, while protesting strongly against partition.

45 Frederick Edwin Smith, 1st Earl of Birkenhead (1872–1930), English lawyer and statesman; supported Carson's resistance against Home Rule; appointed Attorney General in 1915, and appeared for the crown in the trial of Roger Casement; a member of the British delegation which negotiated the Anglo-Irish Treaty, 1921.

46 Thomas Power O'Connor (affectionately known as 'T.P.') (1848–1929), Nationalist politician and journalist; MP for the Scotland division of Liverpool, 1885–1929, and for many years 'father' of the House of Commons; created a Privy Counsellor in 1924.

47 Alan Bell (1857–1920), District Inspector, RIC, 1879–98; Resident Magistrate, 1898–1920; investigated Sinn Féin funds, 1920.

48 Kevin Barry (1902–20), medical student and Irish Volunteer, hanged in 1920 for his part in an attack on a British army bread van. His death became the subject of a famous nationalist ballad.

49 Daniel Hoey, Detective Constable with the Dublin Metropolitan Police, who was shot dead on Townsend Street, 12 September 1919.

50 John Barton, Detective Sergeant with the Dublin Metropolitan Police, shot and wounded in College Street, 29 November 1919; he died later in hospital. He appears to have given evidence against Joseph Plunkett, one of the leaders in the 1916 Rising and was therefore a marked man.

51 Sir John Anderson (1882–1958), civil servant and Conservative politician; Joint Under-Secretary for Ireland, 1920–21; created Viscount Waverley in 1952.

52 Terence MacSwiney (1879–1920), one of the founders of the Cork Volunteers and publisher of *Fianna Fáil*; elected Lord Mayor of Cork in 1920; arrested on 12 August 1920, and died in Brixton Jail after seventy-four days on hunger-strike (not sixty-nine days as stated by Magill).

53 Rt Hon. Sir Laming Worthington-Evans, 1st Bart (1868–1931), Conservative politician; served as Parliamentary Secretary to several ministers, 1915–18, and subsequently held various cabinet posts, including Secretary of State for War, 1921–22 and 1924–29; a member of the British delegation which negotiated the Anglo-Irish Treaty, 1921.

54 Air Commodore Rt Hon. William Wedgwood Benn (1877–1960), Liberal and later Labour politician; Junior Lord of the Treasury and Liberal Whip, 1910–15; Secretary of State for India, 1929–31; decorated numerous times for valour in the First World War, he also served as Vice-President of the Allied Control Commission, 1943–44, and as Secretary of State for Air, 1945–46; created 1st Viscount Stansgate in 1941.

55 Sir Frederick Francis Liddell (1865–1950), First Parliamentary Counsel, 1917–28; Counsel to the Speaker, 1928–43.

56 Major George Arthur Harris (1879–1935), appointed Assistant Secretary, Ministry of Home Affairs, Northern Ireland, in 1921; appointed Permanent Secretary in 1927.

57 Sir James Craig (1871–1940), first Prime Minister of Northern Ireland, 1921–40; created Viscount Craigavon in 1927.

58 Rt Hon. Sir William Moore, 1st Bart (1864–1944), jurist and Unionist MP for

Notes to Narrative 87

North Antrim, 1899–1906, and North Armagh, 1906–17; Lord Justice of Appeal in the Supreme Court of Northern Ireland, 1921–25; Lord Chief Justice, 1925–37.

59 William Thomas Cosgrave (1880–1965), revolutionary and statesman; fought in the 1916 Rising and was imprisoned for a year; supported the Anglo-Irish Treaty of 1921; President of the Executive Council, 1922–32.

60 Eamon de Valera (1882–1975), American-born revolutionary and statesman; sentenced to death after the 1916 Rising, but reprieved; entered the Dáil with his party, Fianna Fáil, in 1927, forming his first government in 1932. As President of the Executive Council (subsequently Taoiseach) and later President of Ireland, he dominated Irish politics for much of the next forty years.

61 Sir Heffernan James Fritz Considine (1846–1912), Resident Magistrate for Cork, Kerry, Kilkenny and other counties, 1882–1900; Deputy Inspector-General, RIC, 1900.

62 William John Twaddell (d. 1922), draper, Orangeman, Freemason, temperance leader and Stormont MP for West Belfast, 1921–22; murdered by the IRA.

63 Rory [Roderick] O'Connor (1883–1922), member of the Irish Republican Brotherhood; wounded in the 1916 Rising; Director of Engineering, Irish Volunteers, during the War of Independence; one of four Republicans executed after the assassination of Seán Hales, TD.

64 Robert Erskine Childers (1870–1922), author of the acclaimed early spy novel *The Riddle of the Sands*; served in the Royal Navy in the First World War; represented Kildare–Wicklow in the Second Dáil, 1921–22; Republican propagandist in the Civil War; executed in November 1922.

65 Harry Boland (1887–1922), member of the Irish Republican Brotherhood, the Gaelic Athletic Association and the Irish Volunteers. Imprisoned after the 1916 Rising, he became joint honorary secretary of Sinn Féin, 1917–19, and Republican representative in the USA, 1919–21. He opposed the Anglo-Irish Treaty of 1921 and was mortally wounded by Provisional Government forces in July 1922.

66 Cathal Brugha (1874–1922), second-in-command of the South Dublin Union in the 1916 Rising; Dáil Minister for Defence, 1919–21; died of wounds while fighting on the Republican side in the Civil War.

67 Sir Henry Hughes Wilson, bart (1864–1922), Chief of the Imperial General Staff, 1918–22; Unionist MP for North Down, 1922; security adviser to the Northern Ireland government; assassinated in June 1922.

68 Maj.-Gen. Arthur Solly-Flood (1871–1940), military adviser to the Northern Ireland government, April–December 1922.

69 In October 1918 the S.S. *Leinster*, a mail ship, was sunk in the Irish Sea by a German submarine. More than 500 people lost their lives, including a neighbour of Magill's. Magill and his wife had the grisly task of identifying the body.

70 Lt-Col. Sir Thomas Cecil Russell Moore (1886–1971), soldier and Unionist politician; served in France, Ireland and Russia, 1914–23; attached to the Ministry of Home Affairs, Northern Ireland, 1923–24; represented Ayrshire constituencies, 1925–65; created baronet in 1956.

71 Hon. Daniel Martin Wilson (1862–1932), MP for West Down, 1918–21; Solicitor General for Ireland, 1919–21; Recorder of Belfast, 1921; judge of the High Court of Northern Ireland, 1921–32.

Bibliography

Birrell, Augustine, *Things Past Redress* (London, 1937)
Martin, F. X., *The Howth Gun-Running* (Dublin 1964)
—— *The Irish Volunteers, 1913–15* (Dublin, 1963)
—— *Leaders and Men of the Easter Rising: Dublin 1916* (London, 1967)
McHugh, Roger (ed.), *Dublin 1916* (London, 1966)
O'Brien, R. Barry, *Dublin Castle and the Irish People* (London, 1909)
Ó Broin, Leon, *The Chief Secretary: Augustine Birrell in Ireland* (London, 1969)
—— *Dublin Castle and the 1916 Rising* (Dublin, 1966)
O'Halpin, Eunan, *The Decline of the Union: British Government in Ireland, 1892–1920* (Dublin, 1987)
Robinson, Sir Henry, *Memories, Wise and Otherwise* (London, 1923)
Ryan, Desmond, *The Rising* (Dublin, 1949)
Weekly Irish Times, *Sinn Féin Rebellion Handbook: Easter, 1916* (revised ed., Dublin, 1917)

Index

Abbey Theatre, 7
Æ (George Russell), 50–1
Anderson, Sir John, 57–8
Anglo-Irish Treaty (1921), 64, 76
Anglo-Irish War, 52–3, 56–7, 62
Argenta (prison ship), 74
Asquith, Herbert, 7, 8, 23–4, 26, 28
   visits Dublin, 32, 35
Asquith, Margot, 7
Auxiliaries, 52–3, 57

Bailey, William, 20
Balfour, Arthur, 38
Barden, Mr, 22
Barry, Kevin, 56–7
Barton, John, 57
Bective College, 3
Belfast, 61–4, 67–9, 70, 72
   property market, 63–4
   riots, 68–9
Bell, Alan, 56, 76
Bernhardt, Sarah, 4
Birkenhead, Frederick Smith, Lord, 53
Birrell, Augustine, 1, 7–8, 18–20, 21
   character and talents, 7, 19, 22, 39–42
      essays, 18
      humour, 39, 40, 41
      speech-making, 7, 41–2, 60
   correspondence, 54–5, 64
   during Easter Rising, 36–7
   during gun-running, 26
   resignation, 1, 8, 39
   statue proposed, 69
   views
      on Carson, 24
      on First World War, 28, 76
      on Greenwood, 9
      on Irish race, 46–7
      on Samuel, 43
      on the Treaty, 64
Black and Tans, 52–3, 57, 62
Boland, Harry, 69
Bonar Law, Andrew, 38
Browning, Frank, 33
Brugha, Cathal, 69
Burgess, Henry, 10–11
Burns, John, 28

Carl Rosa Opera Company, 4
Carson, Sir Edward, 23–4
Carte, Richard D'Oyly, 4
Catholic Church, 51
Census Office, 4
Chalmers, Sir Robert, 37, 38–9
Childers, Robert Erskine, 69
Civil Authorities Act, 10, 72
Civil War, 10, 57, 64, 66, 69, 76
College Green (Belfast), 62
College Park (Dublin), 61
Connolly, Mrs, 10–11
Considine, Sir Heffernan, 68
Cosgrave, William, 65, 69
Craig, Sir James (Lord Craigavon), 64, 70
Curragh mutiny (1914), 27–8

de Valera, Eamon, 65, 76
Dillon, John, 4, 19–20, 23, 24, 26, 31–2
Doig, Henry, 32
Dougherty, Sir James, 6, 55

Index

Drysdale, Mr, 74
Dublin, Magill's fondness of, 2, 10, 61, 67
Dublin Castle, 4–5, 57–8
　scandals, 5–6
Dublin Metropolitan Police Office, 4–6, 57
Dublin Veterans' Volunteer Corps (GRs), 32–3, 35
Duke, H.E., 9, 43–5, 46, 48–9, 53, 69

Easter Rising (1916), 8, 29–37, 51–2
emigration, 65–6
Estates Commission (Land Commission), 7, 17

First World War, 28, 47, 48, 51
Fisheries Office, 4
Free State government, 57, 58, 64–6

Gill, T.P., 50
Government of Ireland Act (1920), 9, 58–9, 77
Greenwood, Sir Hamar, 9, 69
Greer, Sir Francis, 20, 58–9, 70
Gregory, Lady Isabella, 7
Grey, Lord Edward, 28
GRs (Dublin Veterans' Volunteer Corps), 32–3, 35
Guest, Ivor (Lord Wimborne), 39
gun-running, 24–6

Harrel, William, 25–6
Harris, Major George, 63
Healy, John, 49
Healy, Tim, 4
Henry, Sir Denis, 25
Herbert, Aubrey, 47–9

Hoey, Daniel, 57
Hogg, Jonathan, 54
Holmes, Sir Robert, 35
Home Rule Act (1914), 7
Home Rule controversy, 21, 23–4
House of Commons, descriptions, 18–19, 20–3, 58–60
Howth, gun-running, 25–6
hunger strikes, 58
　Belfast, 74–5

industrial schools, 43–4
internment, 73–4
Irish-Americans, 52
Irish Convention (1917–18), 49–51
Irish race, the English and, 46–7
Irish Universities Act (1908), 7
Irving, Henry, 4

Land Act (1909), 7
Land Commission (Estates Commission), 7, 17
Lane, Sir Hugh, 6–7
Larkin, James, 6
Larne, gun-running, 24
Le Fanu, T.P., 17
Leinster (ship), 75, 76
Lewis, Inspector, 71
Liddell, Sir Frederick, 59
Lloyd George, David, 38, 52
Local Government Board, 60
Locker-Lampson, Frederick, 8
Logue, Cardinal Michael, 51
Long, Major (prison warder), 75
Long, Walter, 9

MacDonnell, Sir Antony, 6, 50
MacDowell, Sir Alexander, 50

Index

MacSwiney, Terence, 58
McTier, Edith *see* Magill, Edith
Magill, Andrew Philip
  background and personal life, 2–3, 13
    birth, 3
    marriage, 9, 61
    religion, 3
  career outline, 1, 3–10, 13
  during Easter Rising, 8, 29–37
  fondness of Dublin, 2, 10, 61, 67
  honoured, 13
  House of Commons descriptions, 20–3, 58–60
  Irish Convention and, 49–51
  in Land Commission, 7, 17
  in Northern Ireland, 1–2, 10, 61–4, 67–77
    assessment of problems, 13
    house hunting, 63–4
    riots, 68–9
  in Petty Sessions Office, 9, 53–4, 55–8, 61
  in Police Office, 4–6
  as private secretary, 1, 6–9
    to Birrell, 1, 7, 17–28, 39–42
    to Duke, 9, 43–5, 46, 48–9
    to Samuel, 9, 42–4
    to Shortt, 9, 53–4
  retirement, 13
    called to the Bar 13, 77–8
  stories of Irish life, 10–13
  studies at Trinity College, 6, 49
  theatre, love of, 4, 7
  tours of Ireland, 9
Magill, Charles (brother), 2–3
Magill, Charles (father), 2
Magill, Edith (wife; *née* McTier), 9, 13, 61
  during Easter Rising, 8, 33–5, 36
  in Belfast, 61, 62, 63
Magill, Marie (mother; *née* Spengler), 2, 30, 75–6
Magill, Walter (brother), 1, 2, 9, 13, 54, 57, 75–6, 78–9
  during Easter Rising, 8, 29–30, 36
Mahaffy, Sir John, 33, 50–1
Mannix, Dr Daniel, 51
Markievicz, Countess (Constance Gore-Booth), 33
Maxwell, Sir John, 35
Moore, Sir Thomas, 77
Moore, Sir William, 64
More, Hannah, 18
Moriarty, John, 24
Morley, John, 28, 38

Nathan, Sir Matthew, 37
National Education Office, 3
Nationalist Party, 19, 20, 31, 32, 51
Northern Ireland, 1–2, 10, 61–4, 67–77
  assessment of problems, 13
  government formed, 70, 71–3
  hunger strikes, 74–5
  internment, 73–4
  prisons, 73–5
  riots, 68–9

O'Brien, James, 32
O'Brien, William, 5
Ó Broin, Leon, 7, 8
O'Connor, Charles, 51
O'Connor, Rory, 69
O'Connor, T.P., 55
O'Donnell, Patrick, Bishop of Raphoe, 9

Index

O'Flaherty, Dr, 75
Omagh, 78
Orangemen, 49
Owen, Charlie, 34

Parnell, Charles Stewart, 4
Peterhead Convict Prison, 73
Petty Sessions Office, 9, 53–4, 55–8, 61
Phoenix Park, 2, 67
Plan of Campaign, 50
Plunkett, Sir Horace, 49–50
Police Courts, 1, 4
Police Office, 4–6, 57
Powell, John, 25

Raphoe, Patrick O'Donnell, Bishop of, 9
Redmond, John, 4, 19, 20, 23, 24, 26, 28, 50
Robertson, Forbes, 4
Robinson, Sir Henry, 8, 51
Rosa, Carl, 4
Royal Irish Constabulary scandals, 5–6
Royal Ulster Constabulary, 10, 73, 77
   Specials, 73
Russell, George (Æ), 50–1
Russell, T.W., 21

Samuel, Herbert, 9, 42–4
Seely, Colonel John, 28
Shaw, George Bernard, 7
Shaw, Lord Thomas, 25, 27
Sheridan affair, 5–6
Shortt, Edward, 9, 53–4, 56
Sinn Fein, 32, 33, 49, 51–2, 60
   in Free State government, 64–5
   murders, 56–7
   in Northern Ireland, 73

Smith, Frederick, Lord Birkenhead, 53
Solly-Flood, General Arthur, 70–1
Spengler, Marie *see* Magill, Marie
Stevenson, Sir George, 38, 70
Stormont, 13
strikebreakers, 45
Synge, J.M., 7

Taylor, Sir John, 18, 56
Terry, Ellen, 4
Tonypandy riots, 45
Trinity College Dublin, 6, 33, 49
Twaddell, William, 69, 74

Ulster Party, 50
Ulster Special Constabulary, 73
United Ireland, 5

Verney, Sir Henry, 22–3

War of Independence, 52–3, 56–7, 62
Watt, Sam, 62
Wedgwood Benn, Capt William, 59
Wilson, Daniel, 78
Wilson, Sir Henry, 70
Wimbourne, Ivor Guest, Lord, 39
World War One, 28, 47, 48, 51
Worthington-Evans, Sir Laming, 59
Wyndham, George, 18, 38

Yeats, W.B., 7
York Street (Belfast), 68